Global Competition
and the
Labour Market

Studies in Global Competition
Edited by John Cantwell, The University of Reading, UK

This book is part of a series. The publisher will accept continuation orders which may be
cancelled at any time and which provide for automatic billing and shipping of each title
in the series upon publication. Please write for details.

Global Competition
and the
Labour Market

Nigel L. Driffield

Department of Economics
Cardiff Business School

Routledge
Taylor & Francis Group

LONDON AND NEW YORK

First published 1996 by Harwood Academic Publisher

Published 2014 by Routledge
2 Park Square, Milton Park, Abingdon, Oxfordshire OX14 4RN
711 Third Avenue, New York, NY 10017

First issued in paperback 2014
Routledge is an imprint of the Taylor & Francis Group, an informa business

Copyright © 1996 by OPA (Overseas Publishers Association) Amsterdam B.V. Published in The Netherlands by Harwood Academic Publishers GmbH.

British Library Cataloguing in Publication Data

Driffield, Nigel L.
  Global Competition and the Labour
  Market. – (Studies in Global Competition,
  ISSN 1023-6147; Vol. 3)
  I. Title II. Series
  331.22
  ISBN 978-3-7186-5625-7 (hbk)

  ISBN 978-1-1380-0220-3 (pbk)

Contents

Introduction to the Series

This book series collects together high-quality research monographs written from various perspectives. The study of global competition is increasingly at the centre of an "academic crossroads" at which different research programmes and methods of investigation are now meeting. In particular, global competition has become a focus of attention for researchers working in five areas: international business, business strategy, technological change, geographical or locational analysis, and European integration. Most of these researchers have backgrounds in economics, geography or business strategy. The series will include books undertaken from these backgrounds on the global economy as a whole, corporate reorganization, national and corporate competitiveness, and the role of the city-regions.

John Cantwell

1

The Likely Impact of Foreign Direct Investment on the UK Labour Market

INTRODUCTION

It is often postulated that multinational enterprises (MNEs) pay above the industry average for a country and that this impinges, not only on their competitors, but on the UK labour market as a whole. While issues concerning competition in the product market of MNEs have been well covered in the literature, an issue which is less often addressed is the extent to which employment policies of firms will impinge on this. Indeed the arguments that follow will demonstrate how the employment effects of FDI can not only be a source of gain to the firm concerned, but can also have serious implications for their competitors.

Much of this centres on the reported difference between MNEs and domestic firms, which may for example be due to MNEs tending to operate in particular sectors, which are characterised by, say, high levels of capital intensity, or different policies concerning R&D. While it is now established that foreign owned enterprises (FOEs) pay higher wages than domestic firms, this is only the beginning of the story. This begs the question of whether this foreign presence has an effect throughout the industry.

This simple introduction outlines one of the major points, but we are also interested in why MNEs may pay different wage levels from domestic firms and I hope to present some of the possible reasons in the following chapters.

The explanations of this phenomenon fall into two categories, the first of which is based on ideas concerning bargaining power. These models assume that MNEs' bargaining power differs from that of uni-national firms due to their organisational structure, while at the same time being possibly more prone to strikes than domestic firms. The arguments here can again be divided into two. Firstly, in some cases foreign owned plants are in a weaker bargaining position, due to their position within the global corporate structure, then wages may be bargained up, leading in the traditional way to a shift in factor proportions increasing the capital/labour ratio and improving labour productivity. Secondly, wages are higher for other reasons explained in the bargaining model, or because MNEs wish to "buy" industrial peace, this they can afford to do because of higher levels of productivity and profitability. This is similar to the argument that, irrespective of nationality, the more successful firms pay higher wages in order to attract the better workers.

The second type of study follows the analysis introduced by Hymer (1966). The focus here is on the 'level of production', the extent to which new technology is employed and production linked to research and development, as distinct from merely assembly operations.

Firms who wish to compete in terms of new technology will set up an R&D function in those locations that have a good reputation for R&D, so that they hope to gain from the degree of diffusion that will occur, as well as from the proven R&D infrastructure.

This obviously focuses on the effect that technological progress will have, while factor proportions are seen to be fixed and productivity is raised through this technological improvement. Thus, as productivity rises, wages are seen to follow, but the important question is whether these wage rate increases keep pace with the productivity increases that are experienced by the firm. This therefore provides a possible explanation of inter-firm wage differences. Those plants that have high levels of R&D will have faster rates of technological advance, and therefore greater productivity and hence higher wages. Mere assembly plants on the other hand, with lower levels of R&D and therefore lower productivity, will pay lower wages.

This generates the 'cumulative causation' theory, where production agglomerates at certain sites, with the most dynamic locations attracting the plants with the newest technology, while the rest tend to stagnate. Thus, the strongest, most successful firms are drawn to the best locations, and a cycle of 'cumulative causation' begins. This also has the effect of drawing these firms away from other areas, relegating them to assembly-type operations with little R&D and no fundamental research.

The work that has been carried out on the cumulative causation ideas follows Hymer's theory on agglomeration. Such agglomeration can be explained, at least in part by the technological accumulation of global firms, together with their R&D policy. All technology acquired in a location is at least in part specific to that plant, due to the previous work on which it is based, the skills of the domestic workers and the specific demands of customers. Traditional MNE theory states that in general the most efficient way to transport technology across national boundaries is foreign production, at which point more (local) R&D is required in order to transplant it to the local market and infrastructure. It is this that will encourage firms to centre R&D activities at their largest plants, therefore encouraging technological accumulation, and where this is done by all or many of the largest firms they will all be centred around the same area. It is also a feature of global firms that they create national productive networks, encouraging a system where the plants with R&D at the head, and all others being little more than assembly units. In general, it is presumed that MNEs invest less in R&D in the host countries than in the source country. The extent to which this then affects the local labour market needs to be determined, although the theoretical link between R&D and pay is clear, that R&D will be undertaken in the 'high level' production locations, where the firm employs workers with a high marginal productivity of labour. The issue of causality between the two however is a different matter. This again forms part of the cumulative causation theories which are further discussed below.

International production therefore is explained in these terms, where due to the nature of the industry, a firm has to compete using technology, in the production process either to cut costs or to produce a better product. This, as Cantwell suggests, will lead to an increase in international production as firms have to move to the centres of R&D in order to survive, and will be accompanied by a decentralisation of R&D on a global scale, but a large degree of centralisation on a national scale.

These ideas on international production, particularly the latter, have direct relevance to the labour market, specifically to the welfare of such companies' employees. The most obvious link between the two is the work done by Hymer on uneven development. Hymer postulated that as firms became larger, about 500 companies (of which about 300 would be American and 200 European or Japanese) would establish themselves, and the world economy would strongly resemble that of the USA. He said that three levels of business activity would become distinct:

Level 1 – The strategic decision making functions which would only be located in the major capital cities of the world.
Level 2 – The day-to-day running of the firm with an office in every country in which the MNE operates.
Level 3 – The lowest level which would be spread all over the globe.

Hymer stated that as a result of this, the best administrators, scientists, etc., would be attracted to the major centres and the best jobs, and the local residents would also benefit from the better employment. Those that did not move to the major centres became better off at a much slower rate if at all, doing jobs with lower levels of productivity and payment. It should be stressed here that it is not technology that is creating the problem, but the organisation of the firms, promoting hierarchies rather than equality.

It should be pointed out at this juncture that Hymer was essentially concerned with information flows and organisation in mind, and also that since then the relative importance of Europe and Japan has increased. One can clearly see the relevance of this to the question, particularly from the point of view of the R&D policy of global firms, despite the fact that in recent years the USA has become less important in relation to the rest of the world so the international distribution of firms has become more even.

The New International Division of Labour

As I have already said, there is a link between international production and national labour markets, through the way in which firms promote a specific type of division of labour. The ideas developed on this grew into a branch of the subject referred to in the literature as 'The New International Division of Labour'. Much of the work carried out on this is reported by Frobel, F., Heinrichs, J. and Kreye, O. (1980) and Kreye, O., Heinrichs, J. and Frobel, F. (1988).

The essential thrust of this theory is that with the development of global markets and firms taking an increasingly international perspective, they will locate different (technological) levels in different centres according to the local conditions. See for example Casson (1986). The division of labour within an industry will generate intermediate products, which are then combined to produce the final good. Thus it is therefore likely that firms will locate high levels of production in areas already populated by R&D intensive firms, with high levels of productivity and wages, while the low level production, such as 'screwdrivering' plants will be located in low wage areas with a large source of available unskilled labour. Thus, while this is a likely phenomenon within a country, with such policies being pursued by domestic firms, it is easy to show that the location of the foreign plants within the UK could be one of the most important factors in determining not only productivity but also wages.

In this case, as I have already said, the 'level' or nature of production that is carried out at a plant is closely related to the level of R&D. Where a plant carries out fundamental research the jobs will be of a higher level than where little R&D takes place and the jobs are mainly confined to assembly. Broadly speaking, firms tend to locate R&D abroad when there are locations where host-country firms are already successful in the same area. This provides links with complementary lines of research and encourages growth. Alternatively, however, there may be an indirect employment effect where host-country firms are weak, with little R&D and therefore no new technology. In such a situation an MNE with it's superior technological capabilities may be able to attain a larger share of the market faster than would otherwise be the case. This argument is important because it demonstrates that it is vital to see the foreign owned sector in UK manufacturing, not as a homogeneous block but as a diverse set of establishments, ranging from those which are established in the UK for historical reasons, such as the older American firms Fords and Singer, to the newer Japanese owned plants established over the last ten years. Linked in with this are the ideas surrounding the nature of production employed in the plant. I shall later examine the relationship between labour productivity and wages, but it has been perceived in the past that this relationship is extremely strong. Given this case it is likely that those plants that operate new technology related to the latest R&D are not only likely to have an advantage in terms of productivity and efficiency, but also to pay higher wages. Thus we have a model where it is not only important to recognise the bargaining issues concerning the derivation of prevailing wage rates, but also levels of technology and other plant-specific factors involved.

As I have already mentioned, it is important not to perceive the foreign owned sector as a uniform set of firms. As well as age and nationality differences, there is also the question of how the parent company perceives it's overseas operations, and the role that they play in corporate strategy. For example, the degree of influence that the parent exerts over it's subsidiaries will be an important factor in the determination of employee relations. This is covered well by Hamill (1982). The industrial relations policies of MNEs' subsidiaries depend on the degree of control that the foreign parent maintains, which in turn is dependent on several factors:

1. Whether the plant was obtained by acquisition or from a greenfield site. Hamill found it more likely that already existing plants

are given greater freedom over management decisions than newly created ones.

2. The number of foreign investments that a parent company has. This is often a 'bounded rationality' problem for the corporate managers.
3. The size of the subsidiary relative to firm size.
4. The performance of the plant in the past.
5. The management structure of the parent company. Some are simply more centralised than others, often for historic reasons.

These are all somewhat obvious points in the light of what I have already said, but it is important to realise that many of these inter-plant differences may not be due to inter-industry or even inter-country differences, but simply differences in individual firms on a global scale.

The nature of production at the plant in question may also be a determining factor in this. If a plant is created merely as a screwdrivering operation to service a local market, the local managers are more likely to be given a degree of autonomy than if the plant is an integral part of the firm's overall production process.

The nationality of the parent company is an important factor in many of these inter-plant differences. Dunning (1985) reported some of the differences between the US owned plants in the UK and those owned by Japanese companies. Apart from the obvious differences in the ages of the plants in Dunning's study and the domestic population, these subsidiaries show many characteristics that are true in the plants operated in the relevant source country. For example, the US owned plants experience less influence from the parent company than do the Japanese plants, particularly in matters concerning industrial relations, and while both sets of firms pay slightly above the industry average, there are far more incentives offered in the American plants, than in the Japanese ones, where the employees are generally paid on a piece rate basis, which is assumed to be sufficient incentive.

Both sets of firms however are strictly controlled in terms of expenditure on research and development, demonstrating that in general, the nature of production in terms of product and process sophistication, is something that is determined at the corporate level.

THE IMPACT OF FOREIGN OWNED FIRMS ON UK INDUSTRY

Next we come to the types of study that assess the impact of MNEs in host countries. These are generally presented either in terms of an empirical study of wage differences, or in terms of attempts to determine the extent to which 'foreign' management practices are imported into the UK.

There have however been several attempts to measure the employment effects of the foreign owned firms in the UK. Clearly the amount of employment that is generated by a particular investment will depend upon the labour intensity of production. This is going to be at least in part determined by the wage rate, which will therefore have an effect on the amount of employment that is generated. This is of major significance, as it demonstrates that investment, particularly the labour intensive type with low levels of research linked production, will occur in low wage areas. While this is not surprising, it does again point to certain possible inter-plant differences in wage rates, that will be generated as a result of a positive decision by the MNE to choose a particular location. Of course, if the analysis is moved away from decisions concerning solely the market servicing decision, and introduce the possibility for location decisions to be made in terms of global strategy, allowing for exports from the host country, this phenomenon is even more likely. This is particularly true with firms wishing to move into the European market.

Buckley *et al.* also mention the likelihood that firms in this position will employ a lower degree of horizontal integration across Europe, as they attempt to gain the maximum benefit from economies of scale. By the same token, they are likely to increase the degree of vertical integration in order to achieve the maximum gains from specialisation of production. It is perceived that in terms of collective bargaining, one of the advantages that MNEs have is the threat of switching production in the event of a strike. This would appear to become less important over time, particularly with firms that have multi-plant operations within the EU. What we could have therefore is a model which suggests that a firm will choose to set up a manufacturing plant in one of the depressed areas of Europe, to benefit from the low wages that it can offer, while then being willing to offer slightly higher rates of pay than the local industry average. This follows the work carried out by Buckley and Enderwick (1985), using the Workplace Industrial Relations Survey data from 1980. In an in-depth analysis of the nature of collective bargaining in the UK, with specific reference to the foreign owned sector, they draw several conclusions, which are outlined below.

Buckley and Enderwick test the hypothesis that the nationality of ownership will be an important determinant of the nature of industrial relations agreements, through the role of corporate decision making. One of their major conclusions is that inter-plant relationships within the firm will account for a good deal of the variation in the nature of agreements across firms. More specifically, they assert that at the plant level workers will have lower levels of bargaining power if the firm is horizontally integrated, than employees in a vertically integrated firm. However, Buckley and Enderwick were unable to test this hypothesis fully, and Enderwick (1985) also discusses this at length without being able to test the relationship. This is an issue which I address in Chapter Five.

The final factor in wage determination that I have not so far mentioned, which follows on from the issue of firm structure and bargaining, is that of industrial disputes and strikes. In a recent study Carmichael (1992) assessed strike incidence for uni-national, UK multinational and foreign owned firms in the UK, and concluded that foreign MNEs are more strike prone than any other group. Several explanations are put forward for this, such as the degree to which 'foreign' industrial relations policies may lead to disputes. A further possibility cited by Carmichael is the extent to which foreign MNEs may be the 'strongest' group in terms of bargaining, and thus strikes, the last resort of the workers have to be employed more often. Again this issue is something to which I shall return in the discussion of the results in Chapter Five.

As we know that in general the foreign owned sector operates on average larger plants than the domestic sector, one would expect a greater strike incidence among plants owned by foreign firms. However, this is not born out by the evidence, see for example Buckley and Enderwick (1985), which finds that there are very few differences between strike incidence in the foreign and UK owned sectors. This may be due to the higher wages paid by foreign firms, the fact that they pay higher wages and employ more skilled workers, who are less likely to strike. I shall return to this question in my empirical work. It is of course possible that the converse is true. Strike incidence is used merely as an indicator of trade union power, assuming that a high number of strikes is evidence of strong unions. It may of course be the case that the decision to strike is taken as a last resort when workers perceive that their standard of living has fallen over time, or is poor relative to other sections of the work force. In such circumstances, strikes will accompany low wages rather than high ones.

THE IMPACT OF FDI ON WAGE DETERMINATION

Having outlined the rationale for this piece of work, I now come to the studies in this field that have been reported previously, and an explanation of where this thesis fits into the existing literature.

Several of the early studies, such as Gennard (1974) attempted to assess in some way the impact of foreign owned operations in the UK. The essential point is that the industrial relations climate in the UK is very different from the source countries such as the USA. Thus, any attempt to create labour relations agreements more familiar to the parent company than the employees is likely to change the nature of industrial relations in the host country. We have seen that the creation of single union deals within foreign owned firms has led to a change in industrial relations structures since Gennard wrote his paper, and many of his findings are as true today as when he was writing. Gennard also found evidence of foreign firms being the wage leader in an industry, again something to which I shall return later.

In general, much of the work on the labour market issues of foreign owned firms in the UK has been done is in terms of the formulation and estimation of a wage equation. Studies that address the issue of wages paid by MNEs are often presented with the bargaining ideas being implicit rather than clearly defined.

Enderwick (1985) assesses the employment effects of MNEs, both in terms of the impact on the prevailing labour market conditions, and in terms of the conditions of employment within the MNE. The employment effects outside the firm are divided into direct and indirect effects, which are essentially concerned with job creation or crowding out, and the horizontal effects on related enterprises, such as suppliers and customers respectively.

The next factor that is focused on is the amount of training carried out by MNEs, which through such investment, may add to the nation's stock of human capital. Their presence may also encourage employees or potential employees to become educated, which is usually seen as a common good. Enderwick (1985) sees this as a virtue only if the training would not be available otherwise, and if at some point labour turnover occurs so that the gains are spread to the community. Enderwick also claims that this should only be seen as an outright benefit if the costs are borne by the company, but if the firm's presence encourages people to become skilled or educated then it can only increase social welfare. MNEs' training schemes, indeed company training schemes in general, tend to generate as much firm specific human capital as possible, so that they do not enhance the workers' position in a bargaining situation. To any other firm the worker would be little more than a labourer, despite the fact that the level of labour productivity within the MNE is significantly increased. This is particularly the case in maintenance jobs, where the training tends to very job specific. This introduces the concepts of work-place bargaining power and market bargaining power, issues that involve training, but also the division of labour which tends to generate deskilling. In the same way that training may not increase workers market bargaining power, task interdependency and high levels of indirect (non-production) labour may not be of great benefit to the individual worker. What this will create is a situation where the work-place bargaining power of labour is enhanced through the increased disruption that a strike will cause. This is similar to the argument that Enderwick uses when assessing the effects of firm structure on the bargaining situation. Vertical integration will increase the degree of interdependence between plants, thus improving workers' work-place bargaining power, without the market bargaining power changing, as the effects of a stoppage could be severe for a large integrated company that would find the cost of duplicating productive capacity expensive. Horizontal integration on the other hand may improve the MNEs bargaining position through its capacity to circumvent a strike by switching production.

Overseas operations may also offer a means of segmenting the labour force, enabling the firm to pursue dualism on an international scale. Enderwick talks of this in terms of the Third World, but it is easy to see that this is a possibility anywhere there is a readily available labour force, such as any depressed region of Europe. Enderwick also suggests that firms operating in areas of high unemployment will be able to reduce workers' work-place bargaining power through exploiting the near monopsony situation. There is however, no reason why the firm in question should be an MNE, apart from the fact that, due to their often flexible approach and global perspective, MNEs are better placed to exploit prevailing conditions. This brings in the 'stratification of workforce' ideas of Hymer, where firms aim to create a hierarchical structure. Indeed Enderwick mentions the possibility of this occurring through the R&D policy of MNEs in the way that I have outlined above. However he does not test this prediction, which is something that I hope to do. Indeed, Enderwick produces very little empirical evidence on these issues, and most what does exist is in the form of citing studies that have been carried out by other elsewhere. He claims the MNEs aim to reduce labour problems to a minimum, by using higher levels of capital (although I feel that this may have more to do with the most successful firms wishing to improve productivity, than with the bargaining issues), as well as employing higher levels of non-production labour in the fields of labour relations and management. He also claims that part of the reason that MNEs pay higher wages is that they have a higher tendency to operate shift systems, and therefore have to pay extra in order to compensate workers for this. It should be noted here that, irrespective of the bargaining situation, these last two points are likely, *ceteris paribus* to increase labour productivity, which of all economic variables has the greatest influence on rates of pay. In addition to this, an integrated firm that operates at a high capital/labour ratio will be willing to pay relatively high wages in order to attract and retain the most productive workers, and it is suggested, to discourage unionisation.

FDI AND INDUSTRIAL WAGE BARGAINING

In order to develop the argument from the previous section, it is necessary to present a bargaining model that may be applicable to these ideas. As I have said, the possible threat positions of the parties in a bargaining situation are more severe when an MNE is involved, and this can be taken into account here.

There are several formulations of bargaining models that have been used, both in applied and theoretical work, but they are essentially divided into two types, so called 'efficient' bargaining models, where the firm attempts to maximise some function of its net present value, subject to the actions of it's employees, and secondly the models based on the Nash bargaining approach. Here, the parties recognise their mutual independence, such that any disagreement means that there is no flow of income to be bargained over. For a technical explanation of this see the work of Binmore and Dasgupta (1987 and 1989).

The aim of my contribution is to assess the differences between MNEs and domestic firms, and thus I require a model to determine the differences in bargaining power, in terms of a set of variables, one of which is the nationality of ownership. One of the major reasons for studying the behaviour of multinationals is the perception that they behave differently in host countries, from uni-national firms operating in the same location. It is assumed that in terms of the bargaining framework, foreign firms are able to make an additional threat to simply relocate production in the face of what they consider excessive union demands. However, this is something that I believe should be tested, with particular relevance to firm structure and unionisation, with a view to the extent to which either side is able to improve its' bargaining power, and whether this differs between the foreign and domestic samples.

There have been a great many studies in the area of labour economics that use a bargaining model, in order to determine the prevailing wage rates, but what is required here is a model that will determine and explain bargaining power, rather than use it to explain inter firm differences in wages. The problem essentially revolves around how one measures, rather than proxies union bargaining power. One of the studies in this area was an industry level study carried out by Kochan and Block (1977). They use several explanatory variables to determine bargaining power, such as product market conditions, industrial concentration, the elasticity of capital/labour substitution, and various measures of strike intensity. However, the results are somewhat sketchy, as they were only able to use 2 digit level industry data.

What is needed therefore is a model which incorporates these ideas on the determinants of bargaining power, which then for my purposes allows the sample to be divided into the foreign and domestic firms to enable the testing of structural differences between the sectors. One also requires an analysis of the mark-up paid by the foreign owned firms, and an attempt to determine whether this is explained by bargaining factors, by productivity, or by a combination of the two. There have been many purely theoretical models published on the subject of wages and bargaining power, such as Dowrick (1989), but my approach is based on the use of a Nash bargaining model, to devise a wage expression, of the type used by DeMenil (1971) and developed by Svejnar (1986). I shall return to this in Chapter Five. The final question that one must ask is whether it is appropriate to assess bargaining power in terms of wage rates. While in general, efficiency wage theory assumes that employers and unions bargain over wage rates, and then firms set employment levels, there is a theme in the literature which argues that in fact unions' objective functions are concerned with the wage bill, or the wage share, a combination of wage rates and employment, rather than simply rates of pay.

The above section outlined the determinants of union bargaining power that are used by the authors, but, this list can be widened to include:

Industry structure-(horizontal/vertical integration);
Geographical diversification;
(local/national) Unemployment;
Nature of production;
Unionisation;
Industrial disruption;
Industry concentration;
Labour relations policies – "import" policies;
The degree to which the parent exerts control over labour
relations policies;

Industry specific factors;
Regional factors, grants and wage differences;
Profitability.

EMPLOYMENT PRACTICES OF INWARD INVESTORS

Dunning and Morgan (1981), concentrating on the actions of US owned MNEs in Britain, attempted to assess the actions of such firms and explain them in terms of the characteristics of MNEs. Dunning and Morgan did find that part of the reason MNEs pay on average higher wages than domestic firms, was that they are concentrated in high wage industries. For example they found that in 1966 87% were operating in industries that paid above-average wages. From this they attributed 42% of the wage difference to be due to differences in industry structure.

The reasons that are most often used to explain these differences, according to Dunning and Morgan, are the skill-mix of the labour force, different levels of productivity, and other factors such as different working conditions. These, it is claimed, would still persist in a perfect labour market, but as we know this does not exist anyway, and thus factors such as regional differences, sex differentials and unionisation must be addressed in terms of the employment policies of MNEs. Thus, in order to obtain an idea of whether (and in which case why) MNEs pay different wage rates from domestic firms, we must seek to determine whether it is simply these factors that create the difference, or indeed whether MNEs are different *per se*.

Dunning and Morgan attempt to show why MNEs may be different, they mention the possibility of an MNE importing it's labour relations policies, but in addition a wage differential may be created if such staff demand parity with source country workers. Also, a foreign firm does not have the knowledge of the local labour market, and may have to pay higher wages because of it. In addition, MNEs may be more successful than domestic firms, and therefore willing to pay higher wages in order to buy industrial peace.

There have been several reasons why MNEs may be more successful than domestic firms, and it has often been believed that the strongest structural differences result from the multinational nature of foreign firms. It is also believed that, for example, MNEs are more profitable through being able to exploit the economies of scale associated with larger plants. These also have the effect of alienating the workforce, creating union militancy and necessitating firms paying higher wages.

However, what is important in terms of the positions of the firm and the employees is the extent of the foreign wage differential. There are two basic questions relating to this differential, which need to be addressed.

1. It may be explained due to the multinational nature of foreign firms, as opposed to the fact that they operate in the above-average-wage industries.
2. That the wage differential can be explained purely in terms of a foreign productivity differential.

The relationship between wage rates and labour productivity is an important one, and something to which I shall return in my empirical work. It is important for two reasons. Firstly, if foreign owned firms do indeed generate higher levels of labour productivity, then this is likely to be significant in the explanation of the higher wages rates paid. However, the second important issue is how this productivity advantage is generated. As I have already said, the nature of production will have implications for collective bargaining as well as the nature of the jobs available to employees, both of which will affect wage rates. Finally, the question of any difference between the productivity advantage and the differential paid by foreign owned firms is important, not only in terms of the bargaining model, but also from the point of view of explaining any advantages that accrue to the foreign owned sector.

As well as the technological explanation, there is a further question concerning productivity that is outlined in Cowling and Sugden (1987). Essentially they cite differences in working practices, creating greater work intensity and, particularly with respect to the newer Japanese plants, practices that include such agreements for employees to clean their own work space at the end of a shift. While much of the evidence on this is merely anecdotal, it is at least worth mentioning with respect to any advantage that the newer foreign owned plants in the UK are able to derive. This idea accompanies that of the new foreign owned plants being able to set up agreements with a union to avoid demarcation and other traditional agreements in UK manufacturing sector, although it is less easy to understand why this should apply to only new foreign owned plants. One of the most widely cited studies of the newer sections of foreign owned operations in the UK is that carried out by Dunning (1986) on the Japanese owned plants. Not only do these tend to be developed from greenfield sites, so that the firm is able to decide from day one whether it wishes to have union representation in the plant, but also the firm is able to specify it's own working practices.

Dunning found, perhaps not surprisingly, that there is a very low incidence of industrial disruption among the Japanese plants, and that there is either a single union (no strike) agreement or more commonly, no union representation at all. Thus, Dunning is able to cite a good deal of evidence of worker flexibility in the absence of demarcation problems, as contributing to general efficiency and productivity advantages enjoyed by these firms. However, whether wage rates paid to these employees follow these rates of productivity is a different matter.

While Dunning reports that plant performance is considered when determining wage settlements, the major factor appears to be local average wages paid by other firms in the same industry. It may well be that wage rates, particularly in foreign owned plants do not follow closely the levels of productivity attained. This is again something that I shall return to later, but one explanation of this is as follows:

As well as being able to derive productivity and efficiency advantages simply by being new, the foreign owned sector, has an advantage in terms of collective bargaining. An MNE may pay higher wages in one country, faced with workers acting collectively, but this may be still less than it would have to pay if this were it's sole country of operation, due to it's ability to by-pass a dispute by switching production.

Conversely, there is the line taken by Buckley and Enderwick (1985) which suggests that it may be possible for workers to have increased bargaining power on a plant-level, due to the vertical links within firms. The rationale is that firms that are highly vertically integrated will be more susceptible to disputes in one plant that can disrupt global production. This type of firm may, rather than paying lower wages, (with respect to productivity) will pay higher ones. Very little empirical work has been carried out to test this argument, due to the difficulty of obtaining a good measure or proxy for vertical integration, and also for measures of productivity other than from the UK Census of Production.

WAGE DETERMINATION IN FOREIGN MULTINATIONALS

Buckley and Enderwick (1985) found that labour intensity was greater in domestic firms than in MNEs subsidiaries, and argued that this may lead to higher wages as MNEs will be less concerned about labour costs.

MNEs subsidiaries may have an advantage through their component status in the overall firm. It is often the case that MNEs receive more advanced (in the sense of the stream of production) components, and are thus more specialised, generating improved productivity. Indeed it is believed that a multinational may be the epitome of specialisation, with affiliates being larger but more specialised in order to maximise scale economies.

The main difference between MNEs and domestic firms is that MNEs tend to have centralised industrial relations management through the capacity to leave a country altogether if workers demand too much. The ability of the firm to use this as a credible threat is something that is extremely difficult to test.

The final study that I wish to mention concerning the determination of wage rates was carried out by Blanchflower (1986). This is a key paper in the field because it is one of the first to include in the wage equation a 'foreign' dummy variable, testing for the foreign effect. This is not a central issue in Blanchflowers' work, as it is mainly concerned with the interactions between union bargaining power, and firms' market power. While the results concerning this variable are not reported in this paper, it is important that the possibility of a significant foreign effect was recognised.

However, even if a positive foreign effect is discovered, this is merely the beginning of the story, as the issue should be why should this foreign effect exist and how can it be explained. I have thus far suggested several reasons for the possibility of multinational firms paying above the going rate for an industry, but each of these hypotheses would need to be tested, something to which I shall return later.

The important issue in explaining the difference in wage rates across these two sectors, is the question of whether the determinants of wages are different in the two sectors. Several past studies have attempted to address the first half of the question using a foreign dummy variable in a wage equation, but it may also be necessary to determine whether the forces which generate the prevailing wage rates are different in the two sectors. This could be tested simply by estimating a wage equation for the two groups, and then carrying out a Chow test for structural differences.

PRODUCTIVITY AND THE WAGE SHARE

I have outlined the likely relationship between productivity and wages, and suggested that while higher productivity may indeed imply higher wages for the employees, the correlation between the two is by no means perfect.

There have been several studies concerned with determining the productivity advantage that foreign owned firms on average hold over their UK competitors, but the most comprehensive was carried out by Davies and Lyons (1991). In this paper they are able to distinguish between the productivity effects that are attributable to:

1. The distribution of foreign owned firms in the UK being concentrated in above average productivity industries.
2. The extent to which the foreign owned sector has an advantage over firms in the same industry.

They conclude that the foreign sector has a productivity advantage of around thirty per cent over the UK sector, while around sixty per cent of this is due to the ownership effect rather than the way in which the foreign owned sector is distributed.

However, this still does not enable us to say whether this foreign productivity advantage is due to the plant level characteristics of foreign owned firms, or whether it is due to the plant being part of a global operation. In terms of a productivity equation, if the latter is true we would expect any estimation of the productivity equation to be different for the two sectors.

The extent to which this productivity gain is not matched by any wage differential that is paid by the foreign owned sector, will mean that the wage share in those plants owned by foreign firms will be lower than for the UK plants. This question, and the extent to which there are differences in the wage share between the two sectors is something that I intend to address alongside other explanations of the determinants of the wage share.

In general the wage share is defined as the proportion of value added that accrues to employees, specifically those that are classed as non-managerial or manual workers. Most of the work that has been carried out in terms of determinants of the wage share has essentially followed the Kalecki (1939) analysis concerning the distribution of national income.

In general, this derives the wage share in the following way:

$$w = \frac{W}{W + (k-1)(W+M)}$$

Where k is the price cost margin, determined by the degree of monopoly.
W is the wage bill.
M is the materials bill.[1]

Kalecki (1954) then generalises this to cover the whole of the UK manufacturing sector.

---

[1] From Kalecki – Distribution of national income. Reproduced in Kalecki (1971).

This general result however is then taken by Cowling and Molho (1982) in order to derive an equation to be estimated using cross sectional industry level data for the UK. Commenting on the fact that there is a widely reported positive relationship between industry concentration and wage rates[2], they then set out to test whether this then feeds through to the wage share, given that those firms that possess a high degree of market power will not only be able to pass any cost increase on to consumers in higher prices, but also are likely to have higher levels of value added through higher price-cost margins. In other words the rivalry between the firms and the workers for this surplus value, resulting from a positive price-cost margin, is set up by Cowling and Molho as a model of "class conflict". They then define an equation where the wage share is determined by a measure of capitalist power, such as the concentration ratio, a measure of union power such as union coverage or intensity, and then other variables that may affect the price cost margin. These essentially are the level of advertising intensity in the industry (advertising expenditure/sales) and the ratio of imports to domestic sales, as high import penetration will clearly reduce the suggested degree of monopoly power from a high concentration ratio.

Thus, what we have is a type of Nash bargaining framework, where a given income stream is generated due to the fact that the owners and employees agree to co-operate, but then the way in which this income stream is actually divided will depend on the relative powers of the parties. I shall return to the bargaining framework in a later chapter, and for the time being merely present the results derived by Cowling and Molho, from the equation estimated using industry level data at the "three digit" level. Essentially Cowling and Molho find that the degree of concentration has a significantly negative effect on the wage share, as does the advertising intensity variable. They find some evidence of the unions ability to increase the wage share, particularly when using union coverage data, and insignificant results for the import penetration variable. This model then is set up as a representation of class conflict, which I feel is unnecessarily confrontationalist in its inception, and was challenged on these grounds by Brush and Crane (1984), who included a capital stock variable. However, I feel that this, is a more realistic evaluation of the forces that determine the wage share. Clearly something such

---

[2] See for example Hood and Rees (1974), Geroski, Hamlyn and Knight (1982) and Clarke (1980).

as the capital labour ratio will be important when determining the percentage of value added that accrues to the work force, opposed to the owners of capital.

This chapter has introduced a series of questions, not merely pertaining to the determination of wages in UK manufacturing, but also to the possible causes of differences between UK and foreign owned industry. I have also demonstrated that much of this can only be tested at the firm or plant level, rather than at the industry level.

I have also attempted to demonstrate that, while it is possible to measure differences in wages and productivity between UK and foreign owned plants, one of the key questions is the explanation of these differences, in terms of the empirical estimates of the wage and productivity equations. This hypothesis cannot merely be carried out using a foreign dummy variable in a wage equation. We can demonstrate that differences do exist, but we then need to go further in order to explain them.

An important issue in much of this work is the relationship between wages and productivity. In the area of labour economics, both the human capital and implicit contract theories assume that there is a strong relationship between wage rates and labour productivity, but this is something that needs to be investigated at the plant level. The extent to which wages and labour productivity are related have serious implications for firm profitability, and the extent to which firms are able to influence this is one of the major issues in this work. This is something which is discussed fully in following chapters, particularly chapters three and four.

REFERENCES

Binmore, K. and Dasgupta, P. (1987) *The Economics of Bargaining. London*: Basil Blackwell.

Binmore, K. and Dasgupta, P. (1989) (ed) *Economic Organizations as Games*. London: Basil Blackwell.

Blanchflower, D. (1986) Wages and Concentration in British Manufacturing. *Applied Economics* no. 18 pp. 1025–38.

Brush, B.C. and Crane, S.E. (1985) 'Wage share, market power and unionism: Some contrary US evidence.' *The Manchester School*, pp. 417–424.

Buckley, P.J. and Casson, M.C. (1976) *The Future of the Multinational Enterprise*. London MacMillan Press.

—— (1986). 'A theory of cooperation in International Business'. University of Reading Discussion Paper Series B no. 102.

Buckley, P.J. and Enderwick, P. (1985) *The Industrial Relations Practices of Foreign-owned Firms in Britain*. London: Croom Helm.

Carmichael, F. (1992) Multinational Enterprise and Strikes: Theory and Evidence. *Scottish Journal of Political Economy*, vol. 39 no. 1 pp. 52–69.

Casson, M.C. (1986) *Multinationals and World Trade: Vertical Integration and the International Division of Labour.* London: Allen and Unwin.
Cowling, K. (1982) *Monopoly Capitalism.* London: MacMillan Press.
—— & Molho, I. (1980) 'Wage Share, Concentration and Unionism.' *The Manchester School.* pp. 99–115.
—— & Sugden, R. (1987) *Transnational Monopoly Capitalism.* London: Wheatsheaf Books.
Davies, S.W. and Lyons, B.R. (1991) Characterising relative performance: The productivity advantage of foreign-owned firms in the UK. University of East Anglia Economics Research Centre discussion paper no. 9106.
de Menil, G. (1971) *Bargaining: Monopoly power versus union power.* Cambridge, Mass: MIT Press.
Dowrick, S. (1989) Union – oligopoly bargaining. *Economic Journal.* no. 99 December pp. 1123–1142.
Dunning, J.H. (1985) *Multinational Enterprises, Economic Structure and International Competitiveness.* Wiley/IRM. Geneva.
Dunning, J.H. (1986) *Japanese Participation in British Industry.* London: Croom-Helm.
Dunning, J.H. and Morgan, E. (1981) Employee compensation in US and indigenous firms: an exploratory micro/macro analysis. *British Journal of Industrial Relations* pp. 179–201.
Enderwick, P. (1985) *Multinational Business and Labour.* London Croom-Helm.
Enderwick, P. and Buckley, P.J. (1983) The determinants of strike activity in foreign-owned plants: An analysis of British manufacturing industry 1971–1973. *Managerial and Decision Economics*, no. 4. pp. 83–88.
Frobel, F., Heinrichs, J. and Kreye, O. (1980) *The New International Division of Labour.* Cambridge University Press.
Gennard, J. (1974) 'The impact of foreign-owned subsidiaries on host country labour relations: The case of the UK' In *Bargaining Without Boundaries.* (ed. Flanagan, R.J. and Weber, A.R.) The University of Chicago Press.
Hamill, J. (1982) 'Labour Relations in Foreign-Owned Firms in the UK.' PhD thesis submitted to Paisley College.
Hymer, S.H. (1966) *The Multinational Corporation: A Radical Approach.* London: Cambridge University Press.
Hymer, S.H. (1972) 'The multinational corporation and the law of uneven development.' *In Economics and World Order.* (ed Bhagwati, J.N.)
Hymer, S.H. (1976) *The International Operations of National Firms: A study of Direct Foreign Investment.* Cambridge, Mass.: MIT Press.
Kalecki, M. (1954) *Theory of Economic Dynamics.* London: George Allen & Unwin.
Kalecki, M. (1971) *Selected Essays on the Dynamics of the Capitalist Economy.* 1933–70. Cambridge University Press.
Kochan, T.A. and Block, R.N. (1977) An inter-industry analysis of bargaining outcomes. *Quarterly Journal of Economics.* no. 91. pp. 431–452.
Kreye, O., Heinrichs, J. and Frobel, F. (1988) *Multinational Enterprises and Employment.* International Labour Office Multinational Enterprises Programme, Working paper no. 55.
Svejnar, J. (1986) Bargaining Power, Fear of Disagreement and Wage Settlements: Theory and Evidence from US Industry. *Econometrica*, vol. 54 no. 5, pp. 1055–78.

2

The Extent to Which Foreign Firms
Pay Above the UK Average

INTRODUCTION

The first question to be addressed is the extent to which foreign MNEs do pay higher wages than domestic ones to manual workers. The rest of this chapter will then be devoted to an attempt at explaining these differences, in terms of industry structure, and the distribution of firms within sectors.

The mean wage paid to operatives by the foreign-owned sector is £11343 p.a., as compared with £8735 for the domestic firms, for all manufacturing industries, as listed in the Census of Production in 1989. These are aggregate figures, taking no account of the differing distributions of firms within industrial sectors, but it does at least demonstrate that the foreign sector pays higher wages on average than the UK-owned firms.

Before one addresses the explanations of this phenomenon, it is necessary to test whether this is still the case industry by industry.

The Nationality Explanation

The most obvious way to do this is to estimate the following equation at the industry level, to test the given hypotheses.

$$\text{FORWAGE}_i = a + (1 + b) * \text{DOMWAGE}_i + e \qquad (2.1)$$

Ho: $a = 0$, $b = 0$, that there is no significant difference between the two sectors.

Against the alternatives that:

H_1: a > 0, that there is an absolute mark-up paid by foreign firms.
H_2: b > 0, that there is an proportional mark-up paid by foreign firms.

These hypotheses can then be tested jointly or separately, placing restrictions on either of the coefficients. Estimation of equation 1, the unrestricted form yields the following results:

Table 2.1

Coefficient	Estimated value	Standard error
a	890.24	905.00
b	0.019	0.092

$R^2 = 0.612$, residual sum of squares $= 1.70 \cdot 10^6$,
number of observations $= 79$.
mean of FORWAGE $= £ 9370$. mean of DOMWAGE $= £8735$. Year 1989.

These results would appear to indicate that there is no difference between the wages paid by the two sectors, i.e. that from this it is not possible to reject H_0, that a = 0 and b = 0.

The implications of accepting Ho are accepting that there is no difference in the wages paid by the foreign and domestic sectors, which would appear given the differences in the means, something that is difficult to do. It is therefore necessary to test the result that a = b = 0 by using the following methodology:

The restricted model is simply:

$$FORWAGE_1 = DOMWAGE_1 + e_i \qquad (2.1c)$$

The restricted residual sum of squares (RRSS) is then

$$\Sigma_i(FORWAGE_i - DOMWAGE_i)^2$$

while the unrestricted residual sum of squares (URSS) is the sum of squared residuals from the estimation of (2.1). It is then possible to carry out an F-test on the restrictions using the residual sums of squares.

$$F_O = (RRSS - URSS)/URSS * (N - 2/2)$$

If F_O is then greater than F0.05(2, 77) then one must reject the proposition that the residual sums of squares are not significantly different, and therefore accept the hypothesis that the joint restrictions on the parameters are not valid.

In this case the restricted residual sum of squares is 15.16, and therefore $F_O = 4.92$, and we must therefore reject the hypothesis that the restrictions hold.

Given this result it is therefore important to test these hypotheses separately, that is to test H_1 and H_2 separately.

The simplest way to do this is to estimate the restricted forms of equation 1.

$$\text{FORWAGE}_i = a + \text{DOMWAGE}_1 + e \qquad (2.1a)$$

For H_1 to be accepted in this case, it is necessary that the result here be that a is significantly different from zero. The result of estimating equation 1a from the data is as follows.

Table 2.1a

Coefficient	Estimated value	Standard error
a	1072.81**	166.84

$R^2 = 0.612$, residual sum of squares = $1.71 . 10^6$,
number of observations = 79.
mean of FORWAGE = £9370. mean of DOMWAGE = £8735. Year 1989.
** significant at the 99% level.

The basic result here is that there is a difference of £1000 between the level of wages paid by the two sets of firms. This is due to an absolute 'mark-up' that is paid by foreign firms, independent of industry. This result contrasts with the first one, in that the difference is significant and positive.

Testing for a proportional mark-up between the two sectors involves testing H_2 against H_O, using the following equation.

$$\text{FORWAGE}_i = (1 + b) * \text{DOMWAGE}_1 + e \qquad (2.1b)$$

For H_2 to be accepted in this case, it is necessary that the result here be that a is significantly different from zero. The result of estimating equation 1b from the data is as follows.

Table 2.1b

Coefficient	Estimated value	Standard error
b	0.108**	0.017

$R^2 = 0.612$, residual sum of squares = $1.70 \cdot 10^6$,
number of observations = 79.
mean of FORWAGE = £9370. mean of DOMWAGE = £8735. Year 1989.
**This result is significant at the 99% level.

This again would appear to contradict the results of equation 1, in that there is a significant proportional 'extra' payment of around 10% made by foreign firms.

Not surprisingly, the proportional and absolute differences, when isolated, are overstated compared with the joint estimation in equation 1. These results would therefore appear to suggest that the difference between the wages paid by foreign-owned and domestic firms does exist at the industry level, but that it is not possible to determine the exact nature.

The Distribution Explanation

If indeed the distribution of foreign firms across industries is such that they tend to inhabit high wage industries, then this would account for the large differences in means, allowing for the fact that there are intra-industry differences in the wage rates paid by foreign and domestic firms. A significant positive relationship between foreign penetration into an industry and the level of domestic wages would indicate that the tendency for foreign-owned firms to inhabit above-average wage industries is in part an explanation for the differences in wages paid by the two sectors.

Whether the mark-up is proportional or absolute then requires analysis. If it is proportional then one would expect the mark up to be greatest in the high wage industries. The extent then to which this is related to the fact that MNEs tend to inhabit high wage industries, could act to overstate the mark-up at the industry level.

Analysis of the Foreign and Distribution Effects

The methodology used here follows closely that of Davies and Lyons (1991) in their analysis of productivity ratios in foreign-owned and domestic firms. It is possible to calculate A, the aggregate wage differential for the foreign sector over the domestic sector, using the following formula:

$$A = \Sigma \, X_i \cdot V_i / \Sigma \, Y_1 \cdot W_1 \qquad (2.2)$$

for i = 1 to n industries.

where:

X_i = mean operatives' wage paid by foreign-owned firms in industry i. (FORWAGE$_i$)

Y_i = mean operatives' wage paid by UK-owned firms in industry i. (DOMWAGE$_1$)

V_i = employment by foreign-owned firms in industry i as a proportion of employment by foreign-owned firms in manufacturing as a whole.

W_i = employment by UK-owned firms in industry i as a proportion of employment by UK-owned firms in manufacturing as a whole.

This measure of the aggregate differential clearly includes the two components outlined. The simple wage differential allows for the foreign effect, while the distribution effect is allowed for in the employment share terms.

It is then possible to divide this aggregate effect into the Foreign Effect and the Distribution Effect in the following manner.

The Foreign Effect

The foreign effect can be seen to be the mean of the intra-industry differentials for all the industries in the sample. This is then defined as:

$$F = \mu_{FORWAGE} / \mu_{DOMWAGE} \qquad (2.3)$$

where μ_J denotes the mean sector wage across industries.

It is possible to analyse the foreign effect further, as it is composed of two parts. The first uses the relative magnitudes of the average industry mark-up to indicate whether the wage ratio is skewed across industries, and the second reveals the degree to which the absolute wage gap is skewed across industries.

These are defined as follows:

$$F_1 = \mu_M/\mu_N \tag{2.4}$$

Where M_1 = FORWAGE$_1$/DOMWAGE$_1$: The foreign mark-up, and:

N_1 = DOMWAGE$_1$/FORWAGE$_1$

F_1 is therefore the geometric mean of the arithmetic and harmonic means, and satisfies Fisher's (1922) reversal test.[1]

The mechanism used to measure the degree to which the wage gap is skewed is as follows:

$$F_2 = \{1 + (C_M.C_{DOMWAGE}.r_{M.DOMWAGE})\}/\{1 + (C_N.C_{FORWAGE} r_{N.FORWAGE})\}$$

Where C_M indicates the coefficient of variation of M.

$r_{M.DOMWAGE}$ represents the simple correlation coefficient between M and DOMWAGE. While the relevance of F_2 may be somewhat unclear, it does have an important use in terms of the initial analysis. This analysis also allows for the testing of whether the mark-up is proportional or absolute. F_2 is testing for the degree to which the foreign wage mark-up is skewed towards the high wage industries. The degree to which this is the case will therefore provide significant insight into whether the mark-up is proportional. The closer to one the value of F_2, the less skewed the distribution and therefore the greater the degree to which the mark-up can be seen to be absolute and constant across industries.

The composite estimation of F can therefore be derived as

$$F = F_1^{1/2} * F_2^{1/2} \tag{2.5}$$

Determining the Distribution Effect

The aim of measuring the Distribution effect is to determine what proportion of A can be explained by the fact that Foreign firms tend to be concentrated in high wage sectors, as opposed to the intra-industry differential measured by F.

---

[1] The purpose of this measure is to generate an unbiased estimate for the foreign effect. The factor reversal test, see for example Yule and Kendall (1958), aims to assess whether extraneous factors are affecting the index. For example, what is desirable here is that if the mean aggregate mark-up across industries is zero, then the value of F should be 1. However for μ_M this would not be the case, and dividing by the mean of the inverse removes this problem.

The distribution effect can therefore be explained as follows: The composite of the tendencies for foreign-owned firms to inhabit high-wage industries, and for UK-owned firms to inhabit low-wage industries. It can therefore be defined as:

$$D = D_{FOR}/D_{UK} \qquad (2.6)$$

Where:

$$D_{FOR} = 1 + C_V.C_{FORWAGE}.r_{V.FORWAGE} \qquad (2.7a)$$

$$D_{UK} = 1 + C_W.C_{DOMWAGE}.r_{W.DOMWAGE} \qquad (2.7b)$$

In equations 7a and 7b, the correlation between employment and wages measure the tendency for the two to move together. The coefficient of variation is used to weight the result, in order to provide an overall measure of the quantitative importance of this. What is therefore being measured is the extent to which the aggregate effect is determined by the extent to which the distribution of foreign-owned firms across industries is skewed towards the high wage sectors.

RESULTS

The industry level data described above, generates the result that $A = 1.2104$, in other words an aggregate wage differential of just over 21%. This generates an estimate of F of 1.063, or the average intra-industry mark-up paid by foreign firms is just over 6%.[2]

The results for the estimates of F_1 and F_2 are therefore 1.123 and 1.006 respectively. These results give a further insight into why the estimate of F is somewhat lower than expected. In the case where F_2 is close to one, as here, it may be overstating the adjustment to F_1 in order to derive F. F_1 is a statistically acceptable measure of the Foreign effect, and so, in cases where the 'wage gap' is not skewed towards the high wage industries, F_1 may give a better indication of the extent of the foreign effect. However, the interpretation of the Distribution effect has more relevance if one uses F rather than F_1.

---

[2] It should be noted that this estimate of F is approximately 1% less than if one were to use the mean of (FORWAGEi – DOMWAGEi).

The estimations of these effects are therefore:

$D_{FOR} = 1.0827$
$D_{UK} = 0.8265$
and therefore $D = 1.1417$.

In simple terms, one can therefore suggest that of the 21% aggregate differential, around two thirds of this is explained by the fact that Foreign firms tend to enter the UK into the high wage sector. This then has implications in purely statistical terms in the value of D_{UK}, as the distribution of UK relative to Foreign firms is then bound to be skewed towards the low wage sector. This of course does not take into account the possible movement of UK firms away from markets with increased competition.

Changes in These Effects Over Time

While data on the foreign-owned sector are not available at this degree of aggregation, it is possible to calculate the Foreign and Distribution effects, as well as the Aggregate differential using two digit sector-level data. These data are only available bi-annually up to 1983, and annually up to 1987 in the Census of Production. While these data have only twenty sectors it does at least provide a further dimension to the study. From figure 1 clearly, while the aggregate differential has moved from 1.15 to 1.199 over the time period, the differences between years are very marked, particularly in the early 1980s. What are more interesting however are the proportions of the aggregate differential that are

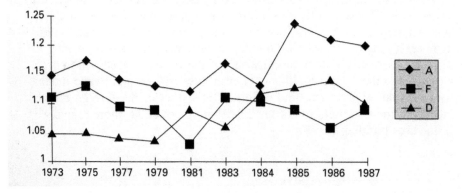

Figure 1: The aggregate, foreign and distribution effects over time

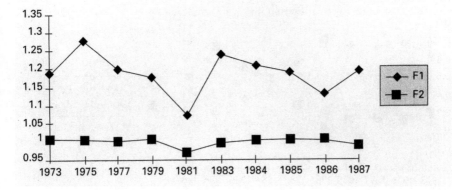

Figure 2: The foreign effect over time

explained by its components. Until 1980 the Foreign effect was much larger than the distribution effect, but from 1984 onwards the distribution effect is on average significantly greater than the Foreign effect. This is a significant result from the point of view that much of the analysis here is presented in terms of the 'Foreign' Effect, which would appear to have diminished over time. The reasons for this are clear. From figure 3a while F_1 has been variable, D_F has increased through the second half of the time period. D_F measures the distribution of foreign firms in high-wage, relative to low-wage industries. This, it would appear, has increased, both in absolute terms and therefore in its importance in determining the aggregate differential. This change in the distribution of foreign-owned firms in UK industry, relative to the domestic sector, has

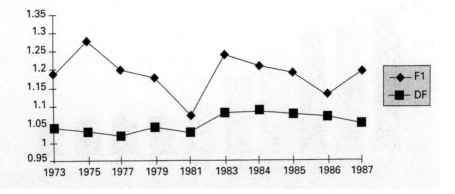

Figure 3a: Changes in the major components

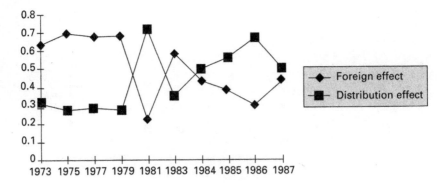

Figure 3b: The relative importance of the determinants of A over time

been accompanied by a general decrease in the number of people employed in the manufacturing sector. Figure 3b illustrates clearly the breakdown over time of the factors determining the aggregate differential. At the start of the period the foreign effect was dominant, but over time, the distribution effect has become more important, suggesting along with the changes in the country breakdown of foreign ownership, a change in the industry distribution of foreign-owned firms in the UK. This is not surprising, as there has been an increase in the foreign presence (apart from the USA) over the time period, with new firms entering the UK. It is therefore reasonable to expect that new entrants will be active in the more dynamic industries with greater levels of productivity, and therefore wages.

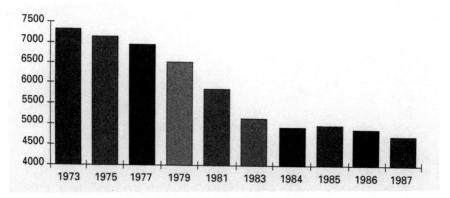

Figure 4: UK manual employment in manufacturing

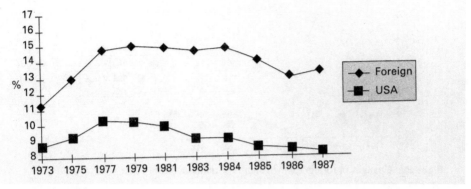

Figure 5: Foreign-owned shares of UK-owned manufacturing as a share of UK total employment

As figure 4 indicates, manual employment has fallen from over 7.25 million people, to just over 4.6 million, while the foreign share by employment has risen over the time period, (with only a slight dip between 1984 and 1986) from 11% to 13.3% (see figure 5).

The most represented source country in the UK is the United States, averaging around 8% of total manufacturing or more than 60% of all foreign-owned firms over the period. The percentage of foreign employment that is accounted for by US firms has however diminished since 1973, from around 75% to just over 60% in 1987. It is this result that may be significant in terms of explaining the variations in the Foreign and Distribution effects over the period.

ANALYSIS BY NATIONALITY

It is possible to demonstrate the above phenomenon using figure 5, with the percentage of workers employed by US firms in the UK diminishing, along with the general trend in the reduction in size of the manufacturing sector. Many of the US companies in the UK are over 30 years old, and operate in the more traditional manufacturing industries. It is therefore likely that an erosion of the manufacturing sector that occurred through the first half of the 1980s, will have reduced the US-owned operations at least in line with the UK average. Conversely, the proportion of employment in the UK by firms from other source countries has risen significantly over the period. This is illustrated in figure 6. Although American

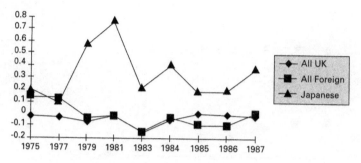

Figure 6a: Changes in foreign-owned shares of manufacturing in the UK

firms still have the largest foreign presence, the foreign sector became much more diverse in terms of ownership over the 15 years covered.

While the data on foreign activity by sector and nationality are not as comprehensive as that used thus far, it is still possible to calculate some of these ratios, and to do a comparison by source country for the foreign-owned sector. The only population data that is available on foreign-owned firms in the UK, and distinguishes between country of ownership, is aggregated across all manufacturing sectors. This therefore only allows for estimates of the wage gap similar to A to be generated for separate nationalities, but this at least does give an insight into the differences in this area between firms of one nationality and another.

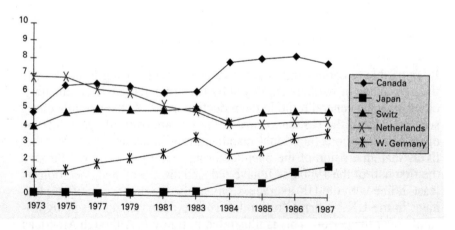

Figure 6b: Foreign shares as a percentage of the foreign total

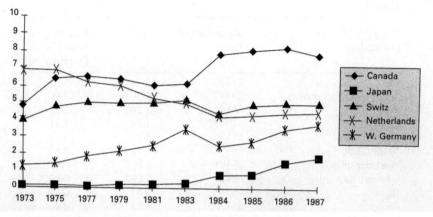

Figure 7: Estimates of A* for various countries of ownership

Using data pertaining to firms owned in various countries, it is possible the aggregate differential for each of the countries, using an estimate of A*, defined as follows:

$$A^* = (FORPAYi/FOREMPi)/(UKPAY/UKEMP)$$

Where:

FORPAYi = Total UK manual pay in firms of source country i.
FOREMPi = Operatives employed in firms of source country i.
UKPAY = Total manual pay in UK-owned firms.
UKEMP = Total operatives employment in UK-owned firms.

Across all manufacturing sectors. This is slightly different from the previous estimates of either A or F1, but this is due to the aggregate nature of the data available. (This measure however does pass the Fisher reversal test as outlined in note one)

For 1986, these are as given in Table 2.2.

The characteristics of the Foreign sector as a whole mirror so closely those of the North American companies, due to their dominance in terms of share of the foreign-owned sector. Despite the results which indicate that foreign-owned firms do pay higher wages in the UK than domestic ones, this does not apply to firms from Japan. From this aggregated data Japanese firms would appear to pay only 87% of the UK average to their manual employees. Figure 6 shows that the Japanese presence in UK has increased over the time period, and is continuing to do so. Unfortunately,

Table 2.2

Country of Ownership	Mean Annual Wage	A*	Percentage of Total UK Employment
UK	£7770	——	
All Foreign Enterprises	£9347	1.203	13.00
USA	£8566	1.207	8.25
Canada	£10412	1.34	1.11
All EEC	£8566	1.102	1.93
Netherlands	£8754	1.127	0.60
West Germany	£8391	1.080	0.42
Switzerland	£8416	1.083	0.66
Japan	£6773	0.871	0.16
Australia	£14705	1.893	0.27

there is no way of calculating values of F and D for each country of ownership, as the data are not available, but it is possible to demonstrate that, with the exception of the Japanese companies, all the nationalities have an aggregate differential that is greater than one, and with the exception of the Dutch firms, employment has increased in absolute terms over the period.

This suggests that the firms that have entered the UK in recent years, as distinct from the older American-owned sector which would appear to be contracting, operate in the high wage sectors but do not pay as much of a mark-up as do the older US firms operating in the more traditional industries. It is this result that accounts for the changes in the Distribution effect and the Foreign effect, which have been greater than the change in the aggregate differential.

It is necessary, in terms of these effects, to allow for the possibility of an age effect as well as the country effect. While it is possible to demonstrate that the make-up of the foreign-owned manufacturing sector in the UK has changed over the time period, it is impossible to determine whether this is as a result of the entrants being newer than the existing foreign sector, or whether it is due to the different nationality of the firms concerned. This measure of A* is an average effect, which due to the nature of the data cannot be examined further.

However, the question of whether the foreign mark-up is proportional or absolute can be addressed by considering the F_2 statistic. From figure 2 one can see that compared with the three other indices this is extremely stable, despite the changing nature of the foreign sector, leading one to infer that it is also stable across industries. Thus, the foreign mark-up is likely to be constant across industries, and therefore an absolute mark-up rather than a proportional one.

Further analysis here however is something that requires more detailed data, particularly at the level of nationality of ownership.

CONCLUSION

This chapter demonstrates how it is possible to decompose the foreign wage differential. Foreign firms do pay higher wages than domestic firms in a given industry, and this mark-up, after correcting for the skewed distribution of the foreign sector across industries, is not as large as may be imagined.

Another important result concerns the value of F_2, which measures the extent to which the mark-up is greater in the high-wage sectors. It is anticipated that this will have a lower limit of one, although it is feasible for the value to be less than one. The interpretation in this case is that the foreign mark-up is lower than average in the high-wage industries. If this were the case one could dismiss the possibility of a directly proportional mark up, possibly for an inversely proportional one. However, the result derived here is extremely close to one, suggesting that the value of the mark-up is stable across industries and therefore an absolute one. Also, as can be seen from figure 2, the value on F_2 is very stable over time, suggesting that indeed the mark-up paid by the foreign sector is an absolute one.

From figures 3a and 3b it is possible to determine the two major causes of the aggregate differential; much of the temporal variation in figure 3b, it would appear, can be explained by the variations in F_1. The other measures such as D_F and F_2 are much more stable over time than is F_1, suggesting that it is the industry level mark-up that is paid by the foreign sector that changes year by year. The nature of the foreign sector has changed markedly over the period of the study; although the US-owned firms are still by far the largest group, both in numbers and in terms of employment, other countries have also been investing in the UK. What should also be stressed therefore is the extent to which the foreign-owned sector is not only diverse in terms of industry, but also in terms of nationality. Therefore the strongest of these results is the extent to which the distribution effect and the measure of F_2 are so stable over time, with the major cause of variation in the aggregate mark-up being the industry specific differentials. Clearly this value is the one most likely to be sensitive to the bargaining power of the firms and unions concerned.

One of the major assumptions concerning the actions of MNEs in host countries is that in some way they have increased bargaining abilities due to the additional threat to re-locate production, (for a good summary of the literature see Davies and Lyons 1988). However, these results would seem to demonstrate that even at the bottom of the slump in the 1980s, foreign firms were still paying above the industry average, while clearly during this period, the distribution of foreign firms became more skewed toward the high wage sectors, as some of the well established US firms in the UK ceased production.

REFERENCES

Allen, R.G.D. (1975) *Index Numbers in Theory and Practice*. London: MacMillan Press.
Davies, S.W. and Lyons, B.R. (1991) Characterising relative performance: The productivity advantage of foreign-owned firms in the UK. University of East Anglia Economics Research Centre discussion paper no. 9106.
Fisher, I. (1927) *The Making of Index Numbers*. London: Pitman & Sons.

3
The Firm Level Study

INTRODUCTION

The previous chapter established that the foreign-owned sector, on average pays wages that are above the norm for their given industry. The aim of this chapter is therefore is first of all to assess this at the firm level, allowing therefore for intra-industry as well as inter-industry variations. Following this then, the analysis will go on to assess some of the possible effects of this phenomenon. To the extent that foreign firms do pay higher wages, it is then necessary to distinguish at the plant level between the Foreign Effect and the Distribution Effect, as outlined in the previous chapter. A plant level study reduces the likelihood of intra-industry effects compounding any difference, and it is also possible to carry out a 'pairwise' comparison of UK and foreign-owned plants, in order to test directly for the foreign effect.

Finally, in so far as there is a significant foreign effect, it is then necessary to assess the implications for the domestic firms in the sector. For example, does a significant foreign presence have the effect of causing wages to be bid up throughout the industry? There are two possible reasons for this, increases in the demand for skilled workers, and workers in other firms demanding sectoral parity. There is for example, considerable evidence that pay bargains in foreign-owned firms are monitored closely by firms and unions alike at the start of each pay-round, possibly the best example of this being Fords. In cases where wages are increased in this way, this may cause a restriction in employment, as firms undertake a certain degree of capital/labour substitution, or alternatively an increase in the wage share, with obvious implications for profitability.

The reasons that are most often used to explain the additional intra-industry differences, are the skill-mix of the labour employed, higher levels of labour productivity, and other factors such as different working conditions. These inter-firm differences, it is claimed, would still persist if the UK had a perfect labour market, but as it does not, factors such as regional differences, sex differentials and unionisation must also be addressed when comparing foreign and domestic companies. Thus, in order to obtain an idea of whether (and in which case why) MNEs pay different wage rates from domestic firms, we must seek to determine whether it is simply these factors that create the difference, or indeed whether MNEs are different per se.

The reasons for this potential difference are clear. For example there is the possibility of an MNE importing it's labour relations policies. Secondly, a new foreign firm may not have the knowledge of the local labour market, and therefore may have to pay higher wages. In addition, foreign MNEs may be more successful than domestic firms, thus being willing to pay higher wages in order to buy industrial peace.

There are several reasons why MNEs may be more successful than domestic firms, the strongest structural differences resulting from the "multinational nature of foreign firms". This follows the argument that it is by definition the most technologically advanced firms that are able to become MNEs. It is also believed that, for example, MNEs are more profitable through gaining from the economies of scale associated with larger plants. These also have the effect of alienating the work force, creating union militancy and necessitating firms paying higher wages.

Cowling and Sugden (1987), mentioning work done in this area by Buckley and Enderwick (1983) and Blanchflower (1984), indicate that foreign-owned plants in the UK pay at least as high as domestic ones. In addition to this, an MNE may pay higher wages in one country, faced with workers acting collectively, but this may be less than it would have to pay if this were its sole country of operation, due to its ability to by-pass a dispute by switching production.

This is how Cowling and Sugden introduce somewhat obliquely, the importance of labour productivity in this analysis, in that wages are only part of the story. Labour intensity for example may be much higher in these plants, reducing unit labour costs even where wages are above average. For this reason, as well as the technological explanation, it is necessary that any analysis of this type should include a comparison between wages and labour productivity. It is the degree to which there is a differential here, that may illustrate the advantages that MNEs may have. It is also important however to focus on the technological capability, as this is likely to be more important than work intensity when determining labour productivity.

Conversely, however, there is an alternative argument that suggests that it may be possible for workers to have increased bargaining power on a plant-level, due to the vertical links within firms. The rationale is that firms that are highly vertically integrated will be more susceptible to disputes in one plant that can therefore disrupt world-wide production. This type of firm may, rather than paying lower wages, (with respect to labour productivity) pay higher ones. Very little empirical work on this has been carried out due to the difficulty of obtaining a good measure or proxy for vertical integration, and also for measures of labour productivity other than from the UK Census of Production.

Enderwick (1985) assesses the employment effects of MNEs, both in terms of the impact on the prevailing labour market conditions, and in terms of the conditions of employment within the MNE. The employment effects external to the firm are divided into direct and indirect effects. These are essentially concerned with job creation or crowding out in direct terms, and the horizontal effects on related enterprises, such as suppliers and customers or competitors.

Clearly then, it is necessary to include a measure of labour productivity in a study of this type. To the extent that wages do follow labour productivity, this will be an important variable in terms of the creation of the foreign effect. It is important here to focus on the level of technology employed by the firm when assessing the explanations of any productivity advantage held by foreign firms.

When focusing however on the relationship between wages and productivity, and therefore the wage share and any wage/productivity differential, a bargaining approach may be more appropriate. In other words, conditions that are likely to influence workers' bargaining power, may be prevalent in plants where the strong link between productivity and wages is not observed.

This suggests that the analysis should incorporate a bargaining model, in an attempt to focus on the relationship between labour productivity and wages, and to explain any differences in the wage/productivity ratio that exist between the two sets of firms. These two approaches should not be seen as competing theories in the analysis, but rather as extensions of the same idea used to explain the observed phenomena. The issues in collective bargaining are discussed fully in chapter five.

Thus, if MNEs do have faster rates of technological progress than domestic firms we would expect to see that the productivity/wage gap would grow faster in foreign firms than in domestic ones. This phenomenon will show up more across industries than across plants in the same industry. Clearly there are some industries that employ technological innovations at quicker rates than others, and are therefore likely to gain more in terms of productivity advantages over the time period.

Hypotheses

It is possible to express these ideas in the form of a series of hypotheses.

Hypothesis 1
That foreign MNEs pay, on average, higher levels of wages than domestic firms across industries considered together.

Hypothesis 2
If this is the case then it can be explained by:

H_O: That foreign firms inhabit 'high wage' industries. (In the plant-level study, this does not arise as the plants being compared are from the same industry.)

H_1: That there is an overall 'mark-up' in wages associated with foreign-owned firms over domestic ones in the UK within each industry.

Hypothesis 3
That these higher levels of wages can be explained in terms of:

H_1: Greater Labour productivity.

H_2: In terms of a bargaining framework.

Hypothesis 4
That the productivity difference (if one exists) can be explained by:–

H_1: Being directly attributable to directly measurable characteristics of the foreign-owned plants in the UK.

H_2: The advantage that may be derived through "the multinational nature of foreign firms".

Hypothesis 5
H_O: The fact that MNEs pay higher wages than domestic ones causes a bidding up of wage rates in the domestic sector. This can be tested by using the wage share. For this hypothesis to prove correct, the

proportion of value added that accrues to workers in UK-owned firms should be higher, the greater the participation of foreign-owned firms in the industry.

These hypotheses that are derived from the theory can be used in order to generate ones that can be tested.

The first of these is tested extensively in the previous chapter, and the data used here provide similar evidence. Indeed, the average hourly rates for the manual workers in the sample were as follows:

Mean for foreign sample = £3.71/hour.   72 observations.
Mean for domestic sample = £3.54/hour.   355 observations.

This would seem to indicate that, on average, foreign-owned firms pay 17p per hour, or just under 5%, more than domestic firms.

THE PRODUCTIVITY EXPLANATION

The next step in the analysis is to examine the alternative explanation of this difference in wage rates. This investigation is concerned with differences between two similar firms, such that any difference in wage rates must therefore result from inter-firm differences, or possibly regional factors, rather than industry level characteristics.

The relationship between wages and labour productivity is well documented, and therefore the first question that one must ask is whether the higher wages are due to higher levels of labour productivity.

The mean figures for labour productivity for the two sets are then as follows:

£ 12091 per year for foreign-owned plants. 72 observations.
£ 10397 per year for domestic plants. 355 observations.

In other words a 16.3% advantage, on average for the foreign-owned firms. It is therefore possible to demonstrate that foreign-owned firms in the UK do have a productivity advantage over their domestic competitors. This is an extremely important result, that looking across industries, that plant level productivity advantage is some 11% higher than the plant level wage differential paid by foreign-owned firms in the UK.

In this sample the correlation coefficients between wages and labour productivity are as follows:

0.19 for the foreign-owned sector.
0.41 for the UK-owned sector.

It is possible therefore, to demonstrate that, while foreign-owned firms may indeed be able to generate higher levels of labour productivity, it does not follow that this can be the sole explanation for foreign MNEs paying higher wages. The correlation between wages and labour productivity for the foreign-owned sector is lower than one would expect, but is consistent with the difference between the wage mark-up and the productivity differential. The discussion returns to this later.

It may be possible to explain productivity advantages that foreign-owned plants have, even in the plants that are merely used for the assembly of imported components. This is explained by Enderwick (1985) in terms of greater support from the parent, and also through the firm as a whole taking full advantage of the international division of labour, making its international operation as efficient as possible. The only way of measuring this would be the degree of international vertical integration that the firm employs, along with R&D and patent data for the different sets of firms, which will give a good indication of the MNEs productivity advantage.

It is possible therefore to see that the foreign/domestic wage 'gap' can be explained in terms of a combination of the two factors, greater levels of labour productivity in the foreign-owned sector, and also the 'static effects' generated because of the nature of the industries that foreign MNEs enter. However, the question here concerns the 'rent' that foreign MNEs earn in the UK. This is illustrated in terms of the greater (than that of domestic firms) difference between labour productivity and wages. This idea brings in, not only the models of competition and labour productivity, but also a bargaining model. This has particular reference to the increased bargaining power that an MNE may be able to generate (when dealing with unions) over a domestic firm.

This may be strategic on the part of the firm, seeking to minimise the potential disruption that a strike could cause, or through single-union agreements and other forms of contract that will reduce the likelihood of industrial disputes, or as has been seen in the UK through the 1980s, foreign firms moving into the more depressed regions of the UK, where the work-force is likely to be more agreeable due to the spectre of unemployment. This therefore derives the outline of a model of wage determination at the plant level. Clearly labour productivity should be included, and then 'bargaining' type variables, and also those which give an indication of the strategy employed by the firm, with specific reference to the plant in question.

EXPLAINING WAGE AND PRODUCTIVITY VARIATIONS

While the main focus of the study thus far is the explanation of the prevailing wage rates, it is necessary, not only to seek to explain wages, but also to seek to explain inter-plant differences in productivity. For this reason, the analysis generates a simultaneous pair of equations to explain variations in wages and productivity, following chapter one.

It is necessary, when formulating a wage equation, to include, not only variables that account for firm performance, and those which will cause differences in bargaining power, but also those which historically have an influence over wages, such as skill levels and the percentage of female workers employed at a plant. There will also, as demonstrated in chapter two, be inter industry differences that will explain some of the inter-plant differences, and therefore one should include industry dummy variables for the relevant industries.

This then generates a wage equation of the following form.

$$MANPAY = a_1 + b_{11}*PROD + b_{12}*UNION + b_{13}*FEMALE + b_{14}*INTERN + b_{15}*SKILL + b_{16}*SEAST + b_{17}*OIL + b_{18}*METAL + b_{19}*CHEM + b_{110}*CLOTH + b_{111}*PRINT + b_{112}*FOREIGN + e_1 \quad (3.1)[1]$$

This question not only centres on the difference in wage rates between the two sets of firms, but also the relationships between labour productivity and wages. For this reason a productivity equation is included, which can be estimated simultaneously with the wage equation.

The most important variable here in terms of explaining inter plant differences in productivity is the capital labour ratio. Neoclassical microeconomics implies that, for a given level of technology, the greater the capital stock, the higher would be the value for the marginal physical product of labour. Additionally, a firm that has a high capital/labour ratio is likely to be more technologically advanced, and therefore have a higher level of labour productivity.

Following Cantwell (1987a & b) it is possible to link the 'level' of production carried out at a plant to the level of research and development at the plant, with the higher level technologies employing better paid workers. Again, the proportion of senior technicians employed will be an indication of the extent to which R & D is carried out.

The wage variable is also included in the productivity equation to test the hypothesis that labour productivity is indeed influenced by the wages

---

[1] For a discussion of these variables, see appendix 2.

paid to workers, as well as the other way around. The expected sign on the coefficient on the MANPAY variable is positive, but the extent to which it will be significant is in question.

As with the wage equation, the FOREIGN dummy is included, to test for whether simply being a foreign firm makes a significant difference to productivity, once all the above factors have been allowed for. As with the wage equation, one would expect the sign on the coefficient of the FOREIGN dummy to be positive, although whether it will be significant is a separate question.

It is conceivable that in both the wage and productivity equations, the FOREIGN dummy variable is not significant. The explanation for this is that the differences between the domestic and foreign levels of productivity and wages are explained by the differences in the other explanatory variables.

$$\text{PROD} = a_2 + b_{21}*\text{CAPITAL} + b_{22}*\text{SKILL} + b_{23}*\text{STEC}$$
$$+ b_{24}*\text{MANPAY} + b_{25}*\text{FOREIGN} + e_2 \tag{3.1b}$$

The ex-ante predictions for the coefficients are as follows.

$b_{21} > 0, b_{22} > 0, b_{23} > 0, b_{24} > 0, b_{15} > 0.$

Using these equations, this is addressing the question of whether foreign-owned firms pay higher wages than do domestic firms. What is more important however, is the explanation of the determinants of wages and labour productivity. For this reason, these two equations are estimated as a simultaneous system, allowing for the so-called 'efficient bargaining' explanation of higher labour productivity through higher wages.

RESULTS

As can be seen from table 3.1, the most important variable in terms of explaining variation in wage rates is, as suggested, labour productivity. The bargaining type variables, SKILL and INTERN are also important, as well as union coverage, which again not surprisingly is the most important of the variables concerning the explanations of the prevailing wage rates. These results also show that indeed some of the inter-plant variation in wages can be explained by industry differences, while female manual workers would appear to be paid less than their male counterparts, even allowing for industry specific variations.

Table 3.1a   The Wage Equation.

Variable	Coefficient	't' value
Constant	2.70	23.38**
PROD	0.000039	7.85**
UC%	0.0048	5.61**
FEMALE	−0.79	−4.93**
INTERN	0.18	1.95**
SKILL	0.40	2.62**
SEAST	0.13	1.66*
OIL	0.38	1.36
METAL	0.24	1.74*
CHEM	0.35	2.89**
CLOTH	−0.49	−2.50**
PRINT	1.04	6.06**
FOREIGN	0.098	1.15

$R^2 = 0.39$.
mean of dependent variable = 3.56.

Table 3.1b   The Productivity Equation.

Variable	Coefficient	't' value
Constant	−3169.9	−3.88**
CAPITAL	0.10	32.40**
SKILL	271.97	0.31
STEC	3676.2	1.06
MANPAY	3080.49	13.54**
FOREIGN	955.87	1.96**

$R^2 = 0.76$.
mean of dependent variable = 10683.
F statistic for the system = 845.58**.
number of observations = 427.
** indicates that the figure is significant at the 5% level.

These results are very much in line with the predictions, and although the foreign variable in the wage equation is not significant, it does demonstrate that, after allowing for the many highly significant variables in the wage equation, the fact that a plant is foreign-owned does exert a positive effect on wage rates. Also it should be noted that in the productivity equation, there is evidence of a significant positive coefficient on the foreign variable. This is a very important result. The most important variable in determining labour productivity is the capital/labour ratio, and while this is three times larger, on average for foreign firms compared with domestic firms, the fact that a firm is foreign still generates a significantly positive result in terms of labour productivity. Given the importance of the capital/labour ratio in terms of explaining productivity, and the foreign firms advantage here, it is a very startling result that the FOREIGN variable is significant in the productivity equation. One can conclude from this that there is something inherent in the foreign-owned sector that derives the productivity advantage for these plants.

The analysis thus far serves as an introduction to the empirical work that follows the issue of the advantages gained by foreign-owned plants is discussed later in this chapter. The next step in the analysis is to divide the sample into the foreign-owned firms and the domestic ones, and then to estimate equations 3.2a and 3.3b for these sub-samples.

$$\text{MANPAY} = a_1 + b_{11}*\text{PROD} + b_{12}*\text{UNION} + b_{13}*\text{FEMALE} + b_{14}*\text{INTERN} + b_{15}*\text{SKILL} + b_{16}*\text{SEAST} + b_{17}*\text{OIL} + b_{18}*\text{METAL} + b_{19}*\text{CHEM} + b_{110}*\text{CLOTH} + b_{111}*\text{PRINT} + e_1 \tag{3.2a}$$

$$\text{PROD} = a_2 + b_{21}*\text{CAPITAL} + b_{22}*\text{SKILL} + b_{23}*\text{STEC} + b_{24}*\text{MANPAY} + e_2 \tag{3.2b}$$

The equations were estimated using the three stage least squares approach, as for the previous analysis, and the results for the two samples are as follows:

Table 3.2a   The Wage Equations.

	The UK-owned Sample		The Foreign-owned Sample	
Variable	Estimate	't' value	Estimate	't' value
Constant	2.67	21.81**	3.13	9.23**
PROD	**0.000036**	**7.67****	0.00001	1.06
UC%	**0.005**	**5.29****	**0.0044**	**2.33****
FEMALE	**–0.83**	**–4.73**	**–0.93**	**2.33****
INTERN	**0.18**	**1.95***	0.16	1.00
SKILL	**0.37**	**2.29****	0.48	0.92
SEAST	0.11	1.35	0.16	1.02
OIL	0.08	0.30	**1.16**	**2.83****
METAL	0.29	2.01	-0.26	0.79
CHEM	**0.31**	**2.10****	**0.52**	**2.53****
CLOTH	**–0.43**	**–2.00****	-1.1	-1.9*
PRINT	**1.08**	**6.55****	-0.02	-0.03
$R^2 = 0.42$.				$R^2 = 0.35$.

standard error
of the regression = 0.64.

standard error
of the regression = 0.55.

Table 3.2b   The Productivity Equations.

Variable	Estimate	't' value	Estimate	't' value
Constant	−3691.66	−4.44	2402.86	0.88
CAPITAL	**0.0098**	**30.52****	**0.013**	**11.93****
SKILL	557.63	0.62	−722.65	−0.26
STEC	1457.2	0.40	5369.58	0.56
MANPAY	**3246.31**	**13.91****	**1666.1**	**2.26****
$R^2 = 0.78$.				$R^2 = 0.70$.

355 observations.   72 observations.

F (system) = 698.79**.   F (system) = 143.99**.
** significant at the 5% significance level.
* significant at the 10% significance level.

Given the previous results for the full sample, it should not be surprising that these results are in line with the theoretical predictions made earlier, as they match closely the whole sample estimates. The one major exception to this is the productivity variable in the wage equation for the foreign owned sample. As suggested by the correlation coefficients given above, the relationship between wages and productivity for the foreign owned sample is much weaker than for the UK-owned sample. With a t value of only 1.06, it is impossible to say that the coefficient is significantly different from zero. In addition to this it is easy to see importance of labour productivity in determining wages in the UK-owned sample. This can be seen through the relative sizes of the standard errors for the wage equations for the two samples, as well as the differences in the values of the R^2.

DIFFERENCES BETWEEN THE SAMPLES

The other differences between the two samples are the INTERN variable and the SKILL variable.

An explanation of the fact that the degree of vertical integration is more important in domestic plants than in parts of foreign multinationals is that within one country union activity is more co-ordinated. For example where a firm is party to a national agreement, it will be dealing with the same union across plants, with that union being well aware of the disruption that can be caused nationally by a local dispute. The amount of information available to unions bargaining with an internationally integrated company will often be less, and the scope for union co-ordination is diminished where it has to cross national boundaries. The relative importance of the skill variable in domestic enterprises may be due to one of two reasons. Firstly, SKILL refers to the proportion of manual workers that are classified as 'skilled'. It is often the case that plants that use skilled, semi-skilled and unskilled to distinguish between jobs are the ones characterised by demarcation regulations and other similar industrial relations agreements, that may be seen as indications of a high degree of union power. These are therefore the plants that would be expected to pay higher wages. The second explanation is based on human capital (Enderwick 1985). It has often been observed that foreign-owned plants like to employ relatively inexperienced workers and then train them to meet specific standards. While this will create a young and highly skilled work force, it is also indicates that the training is to a great extent job related, generating a high degree of firm-specific human capital. This is unlikely therfore to improve the workers' bargaining position.

THE RELATIONSHIP BETWEEN WAGES AND PRODUCTIVITY IN THE FOREIGN OWNED FIRMS

The explanation, of why the relationship between wages and labour productivity in the foreign-owned firms is weak, is more complex. The result that has been derived suggests that, relative to the other factors, labour productivity is less important in determining wages in foreign-owned firms than in domestic ones.

This however, is unlikely to be telling the whole story. Clearly from the previous analysis, labour productivity is an important determinant of wages, but in terms of the actions of internationalised firms, there are other important factors. The previous chapter demonstrates that foreign firms do pay more than their domestic counterparts, and while some of this may be attributed to labour productivity differences, there are several other explanations. In analysing the foreign sample, the analysis focused on the highest paying firms in this data set. These firms are likely to find themselves under less pressure in bargaining terms than are other firms. Indeed, the highest productivity firms will already be paying high wage rates, so may well not have to pass on any productivity gain in wage increases.

A Spline Function in the Productivity Variable

In order to analyse this, the sample of foreign firms is divided into three groups, according to levels of labour productivity.

A spline function is generated in the following manner, to test whether productivity has a different effect on wages at different productivity levels. In this case the sample is divided into three sub samples of approximately equal size, the middle group are those with average labour productivity levels within half a standard deviation of the mean.

Thus the estimated equation takes the form:

$$MANPAY = a_1 + b_1*PROD + b_2*UNION + b_3*FEMALE + b_4* INTERN + b_5*SKILL + b_6*SEAST + b_7*OIL + b_8*METAL + b_9* CHEM + b_{10}*CLOTH + b_{11}*PRINT + b_{12}*D_1(PROD-PROD_2) + b_{13}* D_2*(PROD-PROD_3) \qquad (3.3)$$

Where D_1 and D are dummy variables that take on a value of one if labour productivity is above the critical value, and zero otherwise.

The use of a spline function in this way means that it is possible to test whether the relationship between wage rates and productivity is stable over levels of labour productivity. Not only that, but it also has the effect of imposing a set of linear restrictions on the other variables, such that estimates of the other parameters are consistent across the range of values of labour productivity.

What is being estimated here therefore is the relationship between wages and productivity. For the low productivity plants, the coefficient is given simply by b_1, for the average productivity firms by b_{12}, and for the high productivity firms by b_{13}. Thus, the expected signs of the spline coefficients are $b_{12} > 0$ and $b_{13} < 0$.

Given the results that have been reported above, the expected results from estimating such a model, would be that wage rates do increase with labour productivity, but by less as the level of productivity increases. Given what has been said above concerning the actions of foreign firms in the UK, a further prediction of the results would be that there is some level below which wage rates will not fall, such that the elasticity of wages with respect to productivity in the low productivity group is lower than for the middle group.

The results of the estimation of equation 3.6 are given in table 3.4. These demonstrate that using a spline function in this way dramatically improves the fit of the regression, and that the wages paid by the high productivity firms do not reflect their productivity advantage.

Table 3.3   The Spline Function Giving the
Relationship Between Wages and Productivity for the
Foreign Sector.
Dependent variable: MANPAY.

Variable	Estimate	't' value
Constant	**3.13**	**2.47****
PROD	**$4.3 \cdot 10^{-3}$****	**11.11**
UNION	$2.3 \cdot 10^{-3}$	**3.52****
FEMALE	**–1.16**	**6.83****
INTERN	–0.087	1.22
SKILL	0.017	0.09
SEAST	0.18	0.31
Plant Size Dummies		
50–99	0.17	1.23
100–199	**0.79**	**6.55****
200–499	**0.68**	**5.84****
500–999	**1.16**	**9.57****
1000+	**1.17**	**8.58****
Industry Dummies		
OIL	**1.13**	**7.04****
METAL	0.24	1.82*
CHEMIC	**0.59****	**6.93****
PRINT	**0.67**	**2.76****
PROD-PROD$_2$	**$5.5 \cdot 10^{-4}$**	**11.6****
PROD-PROD$_3$	**$-1.8 \cdot 10^{-4}$**	**–9.03****

$R^2 = 0.62$, Adj $R^2 = 0.51$ Standard error = 0.48.
SSR = 14.71[2].

The signs on all the other variables are unchanged, and the coefficients on the spline test variable are as expected. The major conclusion of this is that, as would be expected, the relationship between wage rates and labour productivity is strongest for those firms not in the tails of the productivity distribution. It is the firms in the middle range that will conform to the theory that is already well developed in the area of wage determination, as distinct from those with below average productivity that face a constraint on how low rates of pay can be offered. Those firms with high levels of labour productivity, however, are already the highest

---

[2] It should be again noted that this formulation passes a Reset type test on the overall specification.

paying firms, and as such do not experience any further pressure on wages. This will therefore mean that their wage share will be low.[3]

Therefore, what can be determined, in terms of the foreign mark-up, is that for those firms with the greatest productivity advantage, the wage differential is by no means as great, and for those foreign firms with the smallest productivity advantage, they are, still obliged to pay a premium over the market average. There is further evidence of this 'going rate' hypothesis. If one takes a sub sample of the top 25% of firms in terms of labour productivity (not surprisingly the foreign sector is disproportionately represented with 27), then while the mean wage paid by the domestic sector is £3.82 per hour, that paid by the foreign-owned sector is lower at £3.77 per hour. This is despite the fact that even within this sample the foreign firms are distributed among the higher wage industries.

These results are not replicated by the domestic sample, and therefore this would seem to indicate that the relationship in foreign-owned plants between wages and labour productivity is more complex than in UK-owned plants. This could well be the effect of prevailing labour market conditions, that wages are related to labour productivity, but only up to a limit. Firms with low levels of productivity still need to pay a minimum level in order to keep their work force, and to avoid disputes, and those with the highest levels of labour productivity are able to generate the so-called 'wage gap' as they are able to pay above the industry average. The highest productivity firms can do this without transferring all their rents to the work-force.

This is despite the fact that even within this sample the foreign firms are distributed among the higher wage industries, with the mean 'industry average' corresponding to the foreign firms being higher (£3.46 per hour) than for the industry average for the high-productivity UK plants (£3.33 per hour). This would also appear to indicate that much of the differential paid by the foreign firms is intra-industry as well as inter-industry. The problem of testing this 'going rate' hypothesis is compounded by the other factors such as the ability of trade unions to gain from collective bargaining.

---

[3] It is also worth noting that a similar functional form applied to the domestic data, produces a result where the estimates of b_{12} and b_{13} not significantly different from zero, both t values being less than 0.5.

ISOLATING THE FOREIGN EFFECT

Thus far, the model has demonstrated the different factors that can be used to explain the prevailing wage rates and levels of productivity in foreign and domestic firms. There are however several factors that are plant specific. Therefore, because MNEs tend to operate, for example, larger plants than domestic companies, this may well explain some of the differences that have been discussed thus far. The issue of plant size is one which may be important in explaining some of the aggregate differential, as derived in chapter two:

For 1988 the average number of manual workers per plant employed in UK manufacturing were as follows:

Domestic-Owned Production: 20.03 operatives per plant.
Foreign-Owned Production: 175.75 operatives per plant.[4]

This alone is a startling statistic, and given what is outlined concerning the possible effects on union activity and therefore wages, could well be a major cause of the foreign effect as outlined thus far.

This part of the analysis is therefore concerned with 84 plants, 42 from each sample, chosen so that the foreign-owned plants are being compared with similar UK-owned ones, in terms of primary and secondary industry, size, and as far as possible, location. This enables the comparison, not only of the results of applying the simultaneous model to the two sets of data, but also direct comparisons of the plants concerned. This should then generate an idea of the 'foreign' effect, because for every foreign-owned plant of a particular nature, there is one, and only one domestic plant of comparable size operating in the same industry. The sizes of plants involved range from a work-force of 13 to over 4000, with every industry possible included. As there are at most two firms in each sample that are included from each industry, this could be expected to generate results where the industry dummies demonstrate a high degree of significance. An important part of the analysis is to compare 'like with like', and to explain, in terms of the differences between foreign and domestic firms, some of the results that are derived from these models.

Applying the model of 3.1a and 3.1b to this data generates the following results:

---

[4] Source, Report on the Census of Production 1988 (summary tables).

Table 3.4a   The Wage Equation.

Variable	Coefficient	't' value
Constant	2.61	9.35**
PROD	**2.5.10^{-5}**	**2.66****
SKILL	0.15	0.45
UC%	**0.007**	**3.38****
FEMALE	−0.63	−1.56
INTERN	0.29	1.73*
SEAST	0.27	0.18
OIL	**0.96**	**2.95****
METAL	0.11	0.45
CHEM	0.37	1.70*
CLOTH	−0.63	−1.57
PRINT	0.36	0.81
FOREIGN	0.20	1.67*

$R^2 = 0.40$.

** significant at the 5% level.
* significant at the 10% level.
84 observations.

Table 3.4b   The Productivity Equation.

Variable	Coefficient	't' value
Constant	−545.04	−0.27
CAPITAL	**0.012**	**16.20****
SKILL	2366.35	1.31
STEC	−1173.38	−0.17
MANPAY	**2715.88**	**4.11****
FOREIGN	524.99	0.69

$R^2 = 0.79$.

These results are very similar to those generated by applying 3.4a and 3.4b to the total sample. The 'foreign' effect in terms of the wage differential appears to be marginally significant, while labour productivity and unionisation are still significant, even though the t values on all three coefficients have diminished. The standard errors for all coefficients have increased, as one would expect with a reduction in the number of observations, which may explain the INTERN variable becoming less significant, despite the fact that the estimate of the coefficient has increased. The position of the plant in terms of overall firm structure was not taken into account when selecting these observations, and so one would expect the INTERN variable to be more significant, if the degree of vertical integration has a positive effect on plant level wages. The SKILL variable would now appear to be insignificant, as the magnitude of the coefficient has been reduced markedly from 0.40 to 0.15. This would therefore suggest that differences in skill levels between plants are very much size specific, so that when this is removed the percentage of manual workers classed as "skilled" ceases to have an effect on wages. The issue of a worker being "skilled" may be either due to the qualifications they possess, or as a result of the job they are doing being classed as "skilled", "semi-skilled" or "unskilled". In either case, one would expect the worker to be paid a premium for being skilled. It is also likely that, as large, particularly UK owned plants will have demarcation rules that classify workers, while newer plants, particularly foreign ones will only have skilled workers according to qualifications where the job requires it (see for example Dunning 1986). It is also interesting that the significance of the industry dummies has diminished markedly, but again in the case of chemicals and clothing would appear to be due to increases in the estimates of the standard errors.

The foreign advantage in terms of productivity appears to have vanished completely when removing plant size differentials, despite the fact that in this sub-sample, the foreign-owned sector still has a productivity advantage of over 25% over the domestic sector. It may be therefore that the foreign productivity advantage can be explained in terms of the benefits derived from economies of scale. It is also possible however, to explain much of the labour productivity advantage that foreign owned plants have, in terms of their greater capital/labour ratio. If this were the case, then given the reduced sample size and the strength of the relationship between labour productivity and the capital labour ratio, it is unlikely that the FOREIGN variable would show up as significant. The CAPITAL variable is obviously the most important variable in determining labour productivity, and is in both the full sample and this sub-sample, on average over 250% larger in foreign-owned plants than in UK plants.

Despite the fact that the foreign effect does not show up strongly here, this is an indication that the model works in a similar way for both the foreign-owned and domestic sectors, not that the structure of the firms involved is the same, or that the prevailing wage rates and productivity levels are equal.

The Pairwise Comparison

In order to carry out a direct comparison, correcting for size, it is necessary to explain inter-plant differences between foreign and domestic plants, within industries rather than across them.

To do this an equation is used to explain the differences in wage rates and labour productivity between one sample and the other, using the 42 pairs of observations. In this case the variables relate to the differences between the values for foreign plant i and domestic plant i, with the obvious exceptions of the industry dummies. The industry dummy variables are included to demonstrate any inter-industry rather than any inter-plant differences. Equation 3.1 demonstrates that using the univariate approach, it is impossible to determine whether the foreign pay differential is an absolute foreign mark up, or one which is proportional to prevailing wage rates. If this foreign mark up is a proportional one rather than an absolute one, then clearly one would expect it, ceteris paribus, to be greatest in those industries that pay the highest wages. Thus, in this case, significant values for the coefficients on the industry dummies provide evidence that the difference between wages paid by foreign and domestic firms is not constant across industries, but will vary according to the industry conditions, with one expecting the greatest mark up to exist in high wage sectors.

The reason for using differences rather than ratios is essentially because many of the variables are dummy variables that cannot be divided.

The full model is therefore:

$$DIFMANPAY_i = a_1 + b_{11}*DIFPROD_i + b_{12}*DIFUNION_i + b_{13}*DIFFEMALE_i + b_{14}*DIFINTERN_i + b_{15}*DIFSKILL_i + b_{16}*DIFOIL_i + b_{17}*METAL_i + b_{18}*CHEM_i + b_{19}*CLOTH_i + b_{110}*PRINT_i + e_1 \quad (3.6a)$$

$$DIFPROD_i = a_2 + b_{21}*DIFCAPITAL_i + b_{22}*DIFSKILL_i + b_{23}*DIFSTEC_i + b_{24}*DIFMANPAY_i + b_{25}*OIL_i + b_{26}*METAL_i + b_{27}*CHEM_i + b_{28}*CLOTH_i + b_{29}*PRINT_i + e_1 \quad (3.6b)$$

The results of the application of equations 3.6a and 3.6b to the pairwise data are as follows:

Table 3.5   Results of the Pair Wise Regression:
The Wage Equation:
mean of dependent variable = £0.21/ hour.

Variable	Coefficient	't' value
Constant	0.31	2.52**
DIFPROD	**2.2.10⁻⁵**	**2.25****
DIFSKILL	1.01	1.86*
DIFUC%	0.002	0.91
DIFFEMALE	**−1.83**	**−3.01****
DIFINTERN	0.31	1.66*
OIL	0.76	1.66*
METAL	**−0.93**	**−2.53****
CHEM	0.42	1.27
CLOTH	−1.13	−1.62
PRINT	−0.58	−0.82

$R^2 = 0.56$.   42 observations.

The Productivity Equation
mean of dependent variable = £2738.17/year.

Variable	Coefficient	't' value
Constant	−17.22	−0.03
DIFCAPITAL	**0.013**	**14.69****
DIFSKILL	−451.71	−0.14
DIFSTEC	−1867.32	−0.16
DIFMANPAY	**4282.19**	**5.87****
OIL	−2349.98	−0.85
METAL	2108.12	0.87
CHEM	**−10043.98**	**−4.97****
CLOTH	6997.25	1.8*
PRINT	−753.66	-0.19

$R^2 = 0.90$.   42 observations.

This system is efficient at explaining the differences between foreign and domestic firms in terms of wages and productivity. It is interesting that the labour productivity difference is significant in terms of explaining wage differences, and indeed given the importance that labour productivity is seen to have in many of these equations, this may account for a large proportion of the difference in wages in the foreign and domestically-owned sectors. The other significant variable being DIFFE-MALE, which is negative. This is interesting given that the proportion of women employed is greater on average in the foreign owned plants

(18%) than in the domestic plants (12%). Given the degree of importance that this variable appears to have in these equations, it is interesting that MNEs still pay higher wages, allowing for the fact that their employment of a section of the work force that is notoriously low-paid is above average. In addition to this two of the industry dummy variables are significant, suggesting that the foreign mark up cannot be said to be equal in absolute terms across industries. This model also includes the industry dummy variables in the productivity equation, and derives further evidence for the 'going rate' hypothesis, in that four of the industry dummies have coefficients of opposite signs in the two equations. In other words, despite the differences intra industry in labour productivity, these are not necessarily reflected in similar intra industry wage differentials.

Not surprisingly given the previous results, the most important factor in explaining variation in labour productivity differences is the variation in the difference in the capital/labour ratio. Again, given the large difference in the capital/labour ratio for the two sectors, this must the main determinant in explaining the large labour productivity gap (29%) that exists in this sample.

The Age Effect

Briefly mentioned in the discussion is the 'age' effect of respective plants. It is important here to allow for differences caused by this rather than by the so-called 'foreign' effect. The problem here however, is that despite the fact that there are numerous differences between the plants that have been set up in recent years, and older ones, the age effect is swamped, particularly by the inter-industry effects. There are however, several characteristics common to new plants as distinct from older ones, that one can intuitively envisage being important in explaining differing wage rates. Indeed, for plants that have been in operation for less than ten years, there is a distinct pattern to the nature of the foreign-owned firms. Labour productivity is well above the average for the foreign-owned sector, at £16521 p.a., while mean wages are below average, £3.35 per hour. These plants match very well to the established view of new foreign-owned capacity in the UK, in that many have 100% union coverage and collective bargaining agreements, but also list only one union as party to the bargaining mechanism. The single-union deals appear to be with either the Transport and General Workers Union (TGWU), or the Amalgamated Engineering Union (AEU), rather than the electricians' union, the EETPU, who, although they have members in at least two of these plants, are not recognised for bargaining purposes by any of the firms. The percentage of skilled workers in the plant is also very low at 9.6%, around half the sample average. This contrasts with the old foreign-owned plants, that have higher wages, although still below average, £3.65, and lower labour productivity, £11984 p.a. Less have structured pay negotiation, with many plants not recognising a union at all. While the new foreign-owned ones are concentrated in the North and North West, the older plants appear to be located around the more prosperous areas of the UK such as the South East with also a high proportion in the East Midlands.

This suggests that there may be differences in the structure of bargaining within the two samples, or differences in the general model between the two sets of firms. However, using sub-samples of the two foreign and UK-owned sets, all those firms that have 100% union coverage (although not necessarily through on trade union), then it is possible to demonstrate that there is no difference in terms of how well the general model for the wage equation works. Although the mean wages of foreign and UK-owned samples are £3.54 and £3.71 per hour respectively, a test of differences in structure between the two samples, using the F-statistic fails using this data. Comparing the two sub-samples where unions are not present, reveals an almost uni-causal model in the case of the UK-owned sample, where labour productivity determines wages.

This outlines the reasons for studying the age of plants in terms of explaining prevailing wage rates. This also has the effect of ensuring that a distinction can be made between any influence on wage rates that is due to foreign plants being newer than comparable UK ones, rather than due to them being part of foreign-owned MNEs. The only way that this can be done is to remove some of the other influences, such as inter-industry affects.

THE INTRA-INDUSTRY STUDIES

These are cases where there has not only been significant inward investment, but also where there are UK-owned firms of a comparable size. These industries are:

Engineering, Chemicals, Food and Drink and Textiles.

The analysis discussed above is continued, using the following equation:

$$\text{MANPAY} = a_1 + b_1*\text{PROD} + b_2*\text{UNION} + b_3*\text{FEMALE} + b_4*\text{INTERN}$$
$$+ b_5*\text{SKILL} + b_6*\text{SEAST} + b_7*\text{AGE} + b_8*\text{FOREIGN} + e_1 \qquad (3.5)$$

The presence of many of these variables has already been explained, an Age variable is now included in order to test whether the age of the plant is important in determining wages directly. It is important here to test for the presence of the age effect, due to the fact that theoretically, both in terms of modern labour relations practices, and efficiency through a newer capital stock, it is impossible to distinguish between a foreign firm which has recently set up in the UK, and a new UK-owned plant.

The Engineering Industry

The Engineering sector is essentially mechanical and electrical engineering, classified as industry 32 and industry 34 in the Standard Industry Classification (SIC) 1980. This covers 116 of the plants in the data base, 25 of which are foreign-owned. (In terms of the representation of foreign-owned plants, compared with 72 from 427).

The mean value of wages paid by domestic plants in this industry is £3.57 per hour, slightly above the UK average, while average labour productivity is lower, at £9856 (as opposed to £10305 p.a.). Conversely, the mean hourly rate paid by foreign-owned plants is lower, at £3.50 per hour, while productivity is £13248, above the average for the foreign-owned sector.

Estimation of equation 3.5 for the engineering firms produces the following results:

Table 3.6   The Engineering Industry.
Mean of dependent variable = 3.55.

Variable	Coefficient	't' value
Constant	**2.9**	**11.82****
PROD	**$2.4.10^{-5}$**	**3.41****
UC%	**0.0028**	**2.00****
FEMALE	−0.38	−1.15
INTERN	0.092	0.63
SKILL	0.37	1.44
SEAST	0.099	0.85
AGE	0.002	0.64
FOREIGN	−0.086	−0.72

Number of observations = 116.
$R^2 = 0.39$. F(8, 107) = 4.19**.

The engineering sector appears to be somewhat unusual, in that the foreign-owned plants pay less than their domestically owned competitors, hence the negative if insignificant coefficient on the foreign dummy. Indeed, of the twenty-five foreign-owned plants in the sample, only eight pay above the industry average, and all eight generate values of value added per employee of over £16000 p.a. This would suggest that there is a bargaining type explanation for why the foreign effect is negative in the engineering sector.

Engineering is one of the more traditional sectors in manufacturing, with high union coverage values for both the foreign and domestic sectors, and as can be seen from the above results, unionisation has a strong effect overall on the prevailing wage rate. The mean level of union coverage across plants is over 80%, while it is significantly less in the foreign-owned plants, 73%. There is little evidence of single union deals being made in the foreign-owned sector, with only two firms showing any inclination towards recognising a particular union. With unionisation being important in the determination of wages in this industry, these figures can give an indication of why foreign firms pay less than do domestic ones.

The age effect here is not significant, although there is little difference in the respective ages of the UK and foreign plants in this sector. The formulation of wages then in plants across the engineering sector would appear to be dependent on two factors, productivity and bargaining power. Within the UK-owned sector, wages are determined very much by unionisation and productivity, with workers merely being able to bargain around the rate that the firm is willing to pay given it's productivity levels.

The equation tested takes the same form as equation 3.5, without the foreign dummy, and the results are as follows:

Table 3.6a   The UK-owned Engineering Industry.
Mean of dependent variable = 3.50.

Variable	Coefficient	't' value
Constant	**2.29**	**4.93****
PROD	**$3.3.10^{-5}$**	**2.88****
UC%	0.0016	0.81
FEMALE	–0.21	–0.42
INTERN	0.27	1.69
SKILL	**0.98**	**2.06****
SEAST	0.21	0.97
AGE	**0.008**	**2.06****

Number of observations = 25.
$R^2 = 0.69$. adjusted $R^2 = 0.56$. $F(7,17) = 5.43$**.

There is the unusual result that productivity is important in terms of determining wages among this group, as is the age of the plant. There are many foreign firms in the UK that have been operating here for years, and therefore will often be subject to the same restrictive practices in terms of employer relations as the established UK-owned ones. This fits in well with the explanation of the age effect, that the older plants will pay higher wages due to the labour relations policies. Indeed, while all the plants that are over 30 years old have over 90% union coverage, the average degree of union coverage accounted for by the most prominent union (in terms of members) is less that 8%. One can therefore imagine that it will be these plants that will be characterised by the older labour relations policies such as demarcation disputes and multi-union bargaining, that are likely to increase union militancy and therefore wages. This explanation concurs with the result that the percentage of manual workers that are classified as skilled increases wages, due to the agreements concerning pay differentials. It would appear that these types of wage differentials are more significant than any regional ones, and that in these cases the percentage of female workers is not important. The extent to which the plant is part of a vertically integrated MNE would appear to have the expected positive effect on wages.

The Chemical Industry

This sector has an above average representation of inward foreign direct investment, both in terms of employment and value added. While only 13% of the plants in the chemical industry are foreign-owned, the shares of the industry accounted for by foreign direct investment are as follows:

Share by Total Employment: 29%
Share by Operatives: 26%
Share by Output: 30%
Share by Value Added: 28%

As well as immediately demonstrating that the foreign-owned chemical plants are substantially larger and generate greater levels of productivity than the UK-owned ones, this also demonstrates that they employ a higher proportion of non-operatives than do the domestic firms.

The sample of the chemicals plants from the WIRS data contains 36 firms, 10 of which are foreign. Again, the average size of the foreign-owned sector is much larger than in the UK-owned sector, with the ten foreign-owned plants accounting for half of the total value added generated by the thirty-six plants.

The results following the estimation of the above equation for the chemical industry are given in table 3.7.

Table 3.7 The Chemical Industry.
Mean of dependent variable = £3.74.

Variable	Coefficient	't' value
Constant	2.54	4.85**
PROD	$1.3.10^{-5}$	0.67
UC%	0.006	1.54
FEMALE	–0.25	–0.31
INTERN	0.55	1.74*
SKILL	2.18	1.69*
SEAST	0.09	0.22
AGE	0.002	0.27
FOREIGN	0.42	1.72*

Number of observations = 36.
$R^2 = 0.36$. adjusted $R^2 = 0.28$. $F(7,17) = 3.43$**.

The chemicals industry is one with above average wages, and while average values of labour productivity are well above the population averages, they do not seem to have an effect on the prevailing wage rates. Indeed, it is difficult here to infer very much on why the foreign sector would pay higher wages, apart from the idea introduced in chapters one and two, that foreign firms pay more due to their lack of knowledge of the local labour market.

A further explanation here is an extension to the going rate hypothesis. While this has demonstrated that within an industry, firms' wage rates will be more closely grouped around the average than would suggested by productivity levels, this may also be the case across industries. Firms wishing to employ manual labour will be aware of the pay being offered by other firms in the locality, and need only compete with that, in the same way that firms wages are closely distributed around the industry average.

The Food and Drink Sector

MNEs in this industry is lower than the average, around 10%. This is also one of the lowest paying industries, with much lower levels of labour productivity than either of the two industries discussed above. Indeed, the mean wage paid by the plants in the sample is £3.27 per hour, and the average level of labour productivity is only £8172 p.a. There are fifty plants in this sample in the food and drink industries, five of which are foreign, which is representative of the sector as a whole.

Table 3.8   The Food and Drink Sector.
Mean of dependent variable = £3.27.

Variable	Coefficient	't' value
Constant	2.46	6.63**
PROD	$2.9.10^{-5}$	1.61
UC%	0.005	2.15**
FEMALE	−0.59	−0.97
INTERN	0.26	0.93
SKILL	1.12	1.30
SEAST	0.23	1.16
AGE	−0.005	−0.08
FOREIGN	0.63	2.1**

Number of observations = 50 R^2 = 0.31. $F_{(8,41)}$ = 2.96**.

Here, one would expect that the Foreign effect would be significant and positive, given that the mean value of the wages paid by the foreign firms in this industry is £3.44 per hour. However, the average level of labour productivity is lower for the foreign plants (£8173 p.a.) is lower than for the UK plants (£8434 p.a.). The foreign-owned sector in this industry is however highly unionised, with 4 plants having 100% union coverage, and the remaining one 80%. Given the significant coefficient on the unionisation variable, this could well explain some of the foreign differential, but not all of it. One can merely conclude again here that the foreign effect exists in this case due to the traditional explanation of firms having to pay slightly more due to their lack of knowledge of the local labour market and the strong presence of trade unions in the factories.

Textiles

The textile industry is mentioned in passing several times, in that it is characterised by low wages and low productivity. It is often the case that there are low degrees of unionisation that is often due to the large scale employment of those sections of the work force that are traditionally not associated with the union movement, such as women and part time workers. Indeed, the mean wage paid in this sector is £2.73 per hour, significantly below the sample average, and the mean value for the FEMALE variable across the thirty plants is 0.49, as opposed to the average for the whole sample of 0.18. To the extent that the low pay of women workers is an inter-industry phenomenon, the FEMALE variable may not show up here. In this case the presence of a high proportion of women workers having a significant negative effect on wages, may be illustrated in the low industry average wage. The foreign share in this industry across the UK is, not surprisingly lower than the other cases, given that the foreign sector being skewed towards the high wage, high productivity sectors. Indeed, the foreign share in the industry, by employment is less than 7% for the whole sector. Low productivity sectors are often those where intra industry, wage differences are closely linked to productivity. With productivity in the two foreign plants being over 50% higher than the industry average, one would expect a significant foreign effect.

Table 3.9   The Textile Industry.
Mean of dependent variable = £2.75.

Variable	Coefficient	't' value
Constant	2.50	7.04**
PROD	$4.4.10^{-5}$	3.14**
UC%	−0.0013	−0.63
FEMALE	−0.16	−0.47
INTERN	0.16	0.65
SKILL	0.05	0.13
SEAST	−0.49	−1.72*
AGE	0.002	0.05
FOREIGN	0.32	0.93

Number of observations = 30.
$R^2 = 0.41$. adjusted $R^2 = 0.31$ $F(8, 21) = 3.06**$.

The one surprising variable here is the South East dummy variable, having a significant negative coefficient. Labour productivity is an important part of wage determination, and therefore much of the foreign wage differential can be explained in terms of the foreign productivity advantage. There is evidence here across the industry that there is a complete lack of bargaining power that can be gained by the workers. There are few skill differentials, or possible bargaining gains from the structure of the firm. This is despite the proportion of skilled workers overall being greater than the national average, and union coverage having no effect. In such cases, the wage share is going to be low, one can see that although the foreign-owned firms do pay above the industry average, the foreign effect is not significant, and the unions are not able to gain any of the productivity advantage that the firm can generate. Indeed, one of the two foreign firms here pays only three pence per hour above the industry average, despite generating a value of value added per employee some 50% above the average.

CONCLUSIONS FROM THE PLANT LEVEL STUDIES

This chapter has addressed four of the five hypotheses that are advanced by this model. Linking the work done here with that presented in chapter two, it is possible to conclude that the foreign-owned sector in UK manufacturing pays higher wage rates than the UK-owned sector. This can partly be explained by the distribution effect, but it is also true for studies within industries. This 'foreign mark up' can to an extent be explained in terms of the productivity advantages generated by foreign-owned firms, but, the relationship between wages and productivity is very weak for the foreign-owned sector. Explaining the foreign effect through collective bargaining, and through productivity are by no means competing hypotheses, but complement each other. Intuitively, workers bargaining power to raise their wages above the going rate will in part be determined by the firm's ability to pay, which is of course related to productivity or profitability. Thus, in the wage equations, there are bargaining power variables as well as firm structure variables and productivity. While the relationship between wages and productivity is more complex in the foreign-owned sector than in the domestic one, it is also true that this is due mainly to inter-industry factors rather than plant-specific ones. Coupled with this is the result that the foreign effect in terms of productivity is significant, even allowing for the fact that there is across the whole sample a strong relationship between the capital/labour ratio and productivity, and that the foreign sector has a significantly higher capital/labour ratio than the foreign-owned sector. This indicates that there are other gains that are derived by the very nature of a firm being a multinational. This is easiest to explain in terms of the technology utilised, and the speed with which new technology is assimilated, and in terms of the labour relations techniques employed.

Despite these differences between the two sectors, an F test for structural differences in the model between the two sectors generates an insignificant result, such that one concludes that while the levels of the variables may be different between the two samples, resulting in different levels of wages between the samples, the ways that the variables work within the model are very similar. This is an important result, as it then means that any differences can be explained in terms of differences in the independent variables, or in terms of the foreign effect at the plant level, which is what the model seeks to quantify. In several of the regressions presented above, the foreign effect is at least significant at the 10% level, after allowing for inter plant and inter-industry effects, leading one to conclude that there are indeed other reasons why the foreign firms should pay above the industry average.

This chapter also demonstrates that any foreign differential, both in terms of wages and productivity, is indeed due to the foreign ownership rather than the age of the plant. In theoretical terms, much of the previous work finds it impossible to distinguish between the age effect and the foreign effect, as a new plant may generate many of the advantages attributed to foreign plants.

The same is true for the size effect, while it is true that the average size of foreign-owned plants in the UK is much larger than that of the UK sector, correcting for this does not greatly change the results, but again emphasises the presence of the foreign effect.

The one subject on which little has been said thus far is that of the inter-industry differences in the estimates. The application of the pairwise model in particular shows up the inter-industry differences in wages in the model, which then must be taken into account before evaluating the inter-plant differences. This is why there is such a weak relationship between wages and productivity for the foreign sector. While foreign firms do pay more than the domestic firms, one of the most important determinants of the prevailing wage rates is the industry average, or the 'going rate'. It has been noticeable that in all these studies, the constant terms in the equation have been significantly different from zero, supporting the concept of the going rate, and giving a meaningful value of so much per hour, with the inter-firm conditions causing the actual values to vary around this. The constant term is often the most significant coefficient in the equation, and is obviously close to the mean value for the sample. This is why all these equations have been presented as linear, rather than log-linear. A measurement for the constant term in each case is essential in order to obtain an idea of the explanations of the differences between the samples. Indeed, it is noticeable from this that the constant term in the estimation of the basic model for the foreign sample is 3.13 (t value = 9.23) while for the UK sample it is 2.67 (t value = 21.81). This is then without taking into account any inter-plant or inter-industry differences in the explanatory variables.

It is this result, along with the pairwise comparison and the model containing the productivity slope dummy, that provides the greatest support for the going rate hypothesis, that essentially a foreign-owned firm will pay the going rate for the industry, plus a mark up, either to attract the better workers to gain a productivity advantage, or to buy industrial peace. The significant coefficients on the industry dummies in the pairwise comparison suggest that this is a proportional mark up (i.e. $b > 0$ in equation 3.1), and thus will, in absolute terms increase with average wages. Clearly then, the extent to which this mark up is paid in order to avoid industrial disputes will affect the absolute size through the relative bargaining power of the two parties, something that is discussed in greater length in chapter five.

The one issue that is mentioned in the hypotheses to be tested, that has not directly been addressed here is the effect that the willingness of the foreign sector to pay this mark up, has on the domestic firms. Clearly, the extent to which they are forced to match any such payments, through workers demanding sectoral parity may have serious implications for the wage share, and therefore profitability of the companies. This chapter has shown that while the foreign sector does pay a mark up, its advantages in terms of labour productivity are even greater. One would expect therefore, that the wage share in foreign firms to be lower than in domestic firms, but the extent to which a foreign presence can cause the wage share to rise in other firms is something that is addressed in the next chapter.

REFERENCES

Blanchflower, D. (1986) Wages and Concentration in British Manufacturing. *Applied Economics* no. 18 pp. 1025–38.

Cantwell, J.A. (1987a) 'Technological Advantage as a determinant of the international activity of firms.' University of Reading discussion papers, series B no. 105.

Cantwell, J.A. (1987b) 'Technical Competition and Intra-Industry production in the Industrialised World.' University of Reading discussion papers, series B no. 106.

Cowling, K. and Sugden, R. (1987) *Transnational Monopoly Capitalism*. London: Wheatsheaf Books.

Enderwick, P. (1985) *Multinational Business and Labour*. London Croom-Helm.

4

Implications for UK Manufacturing

THE FOREIGN EFFECT AND UK WAGE RATES

At the start of the previous chapter, five hypotheses were outlined that could then be tested, in order to answer the questions posed in chapter two. The final one however was not addressed, the extent to which the foreign effect, corrected for inter-industry differences, then has the effect of causing wage rates to be bid up in the industry. For example Ford is a major employer in the UK, and one of the first firms each Autumn to complete their pay bargaining. They are widely used as a signal to the manufacturing sector, with the agreements being widely covered in the media. There are several other large firms in a similar position, and by the nature of the manufacturing sector and it is logical that many will be foreign-owned.

The final hypothesis then, is the extent to which the presence of foreign-owned firms in an industry changes the nature of the industry from the point of view of the labour market. In specific terms, the issue is whether foreign-owned firms cause wages to be bid up across the industry, and then whether this then has an effect on the wage share.

In order to assess this it is then necessary to form an idea of the relationship between the wages paid by domestic firms, and the degree of foreign penetration in the relevant industry. In addition, in order for the any effects on the wage share to be included, it is necessary to test for the possibility of foreign-owned firms increasing the level of industry productivity. This is an important question, as the extent to which average levels of labour productivity are increased through the presence of foreign MNEs is one of the key reasons for inward investment incentives in the UK. While employment generation is often the major consideration, the rationale for giving preference to foreign-owned as opposed to new UK-owned plants, is that the industry and then UK manufacturing in

69

general will derive productivity gains through the diffusion of techno-logical capability, or through increased competition. The extent to which the presence of a high proportion of foreign-owned firms in an industry does cause an increase in general wage rates without improving labour productivity poses a serious question. This not only indicates that the UK firms may be experiencing a profit squeeze, but also may call into ques-tion the extent to which foreign firms should be given incentives to set up in the UK. In the longer term they may be causing a substitution in terms of employment, away from the established firms, and thus have an effect on total UK employment that is somewhat less than imagined.

Thus, the simultaneous system outlined above is modified to form the following equations:

$$\text{MANPAY} = a_1 + b_{11}*\text{PROD} + b_{12}*\text{UNION} + b_{13}*\text{FEMALE} + b_{14}*\text{INTERN} + b_{15}*\text{SKILL} + b_{16}*\text{SEAST} + b_{17}*\text{OIL} + b_{18}*\text{METAL} + b_{19}*\text{CHEM} + b_{110}*\text{CLOTH} + b_{111}*\text{PRINT} + b_{112}*\text{FORSHARE} + e_1 \quad (4.1a)$$

$$\text{PROD} = a_2 + b_{21}*\text{CAPITAL} + b_{22}*\text{SKILL} + b_{23}*\text{STEC} + b_{24}*\text{MANPAY} + b_{25}*\text{FORSHARE} + e \quad (4.1b)$$

FORSHARE is the percentage of workers in the relevant industry that are employed by foreign- owned firms, and ranges from 3% to over 60%. These equations are then estimated for the UK-owned sample only. The results are given in Table 4.1.

Table 4.1   The Wage Equation.

Variable	Coefficient	't' value
Constant	2.61	18.97**
PROD	$3.8.10^{-5}$	7.78**
SKILL	0.38	2.07**
UC%	0.005	4.79**
FEMALE	−0.85	−4.41**
INTERN	0.27	1.89*
SEAST	0.06	0.63
OIL	0.32	0.86
METAL	0.27	1.71*
CHEM	0.21	1.18
CLOTH	−0.39	−1.59
PRINT	1.09	6.37**
FORSHARE	0.56	1.61

$R^2 = 0.53$. 330 observations.

Table 4.1—*continued*

The Productivity Equation

Variable	Coefficient	't ' value
Constant	−3994.53	−4.54**
CAPITAL	0.010	28.43**
SKILL	681.18	0.71
STEC	1021.1	0.26
MANPAY	3352.86	13.67**
FORSHARE	−193.91	−0.10

$R^2 = 0.77$.

These results serve to demonstrate that, while the positive effect on wages that the foreign firms have on the wage rates of their competitors is not significant, it is greater than the effect on productivity. Chapter two demonstrates that the distribution of foreign-owned firms is not even across industries, but skewed towards the high productivity sector. It would appear however, that this is very much a relationship that exists only in one direction, that is that while foreign firms do enter the high-wage high productivity sectors, they have little effect on productivity levels within the industry. This therefore indicates that little in terms of technological progress is disseminated across the industry. The presence of foreign-owned firms can have serious connotations for the competitiveness, and therefore profitability and viability of the UK-owned sector.

ANALYSIS OF THE WAGE SHARE IN UK MANUFACTURING

The best method of testing this with cross sectional data is to assess the relationship between the proportion of an industry accounted for by the foreign-owned sector, and the wage share. Defining the wage share as the percentage of value added that is paid in wages to manual workers, then clearly this is going to be determined by similar factors that explain wages and productivity. Again, the issue is the deviation around the average, that will be determined mainly through bargaining.

For any plant, we assume that there is a productivity/wage differential, that is any gain in labour productivity does not accrue wholly to the employees. However, clearly the actual level of this will be explained by the wage share equation. Having demonstrated that wages do not match labour productivity, it is therefore likely that factors which affect wages and productivity, such as skills, will have a negative effect on the wage share. Conversely, those which have a positive influence on wages through collective bargaining such as unionisation or the degree of vertical integration will have a positive effect on the wage share. The discussion in the previous three chapters therefore would suggest that the effect on the wage share on the foreign presence should be positive.

All the work that has been carried out into the determination of the wage share in UK manufacturing is in terms of attaining an indication of the extent to which the relationship between employers and employees can be modelled in terms of class conflict. Following the theoretical work by Kalecki (1971), into the distribution of national income, there have been a few papers using the wage share at the industry level as an indicator of how the monopoly surplus is divided between capitalists and employees.

Much of this follows Cowling and Molho (1980). Using Kalecki's analysis of wage determination within the class struggle, they determine that the degree of success that trade unions (the working class) are successful in obtaining some of the monopoly surplus from the employers (the capitalist class) will show up, not so much in wages but in the wage share. This is clearly a similar idea to my formulation of the hypothesis, in that while bargaining factors may have positive effects on wage rates, it is likely that the greater effect will show up in the wage share.

Cowling and Molho (1980) were however attempting to determine the success of the workers in the class struggle, and therefore formulate their equation in the following way.

The wage share is determined as, the proportion of gross output minus material costs that is accounted for by wage costs of operatives. Given their formulation, it is necessary to have a measure of the degree of monopoly in the industry, the most common of which is the five firm concentration ratio, the proportion of the sectoral employment accounted for by the largest five firms. It is possible, however, that this variable may work in two directions. First of all it is likely that the degree of monopoly power will increase profits and therefore reduce the wage share, but also possible that firms in this position will be willing to pay higher wages, not just in order to avoid conflict, but also to attract the more skilled and productive workers.

The converse of the monopoly variable is union power. Cowling and Molho propose three possible measures of this, rate of strikes, percentage of man-days lost through disputes, and union coverage. The first two of these may be very firm specific, rather than industry specific, as it is rare for disputes to be industry wide in the private sector, while it is more likely for some sectors to be unionised across the industry.

Cowling and Molho also include the advertising/sales ratio, as a proxy for the price elasticity of the market demand curve, and the degree of import penetration into the industry. It is likely that the five firm concentration ratio will over estimate the degree of monopoly in the industry, due to further competition from imports, and so it is expected that this variable may act against the concentration variable.

This equation was then estimated in log-linear form using industry level data. Cowling and Molho report little success with this formulation of the model, but conclude that the degree of monopoly exerts significant downward pressure on the wage share, with the appropriate unionisation variable being union coverage. In all their formulations of this model, the R^2 ranging from 0.106 to 0.194.

Papers published on this subject following Cowling and Molho have concerned themselves with the class struggle debate raised in the original paper. See for example, Brush and Crane (1985) and Henley (1986). The arguments centre around the formulation of the model, within this framework. Brush and Crane for example include a capital intensity variable, which they find to have a highly significant negative effect on the wage share. This makes intuitive sense, as one would expect the level of the wage share to fall with any increase in the capital/labour ratio.

While not wishing to be too far removed from the idea that interactions between unions and employers will be important in the determinants of the wage share, The purpose here is not to devise a model of class conflict in the Cowling tradition. While the point of interest here, is still the share of value added that accrues to workers, it is for different reasons. With particular reference to the foreign-owned sector, these firms have a productivity advantage that is much larger than the wage differential paid, and therefore one would expect the wage share to be lower in the foreign-owned sector. While it may be the case that the share of value added that is paid in wages is lower than for the domestic sector, this is not explained in terms of monopoly profits as in the Cowling model. The aim of my piece of work is therefore to determine how effective workers are in attaining gains that are available from any productivity advantage accruing to the foreign-owned firms in an industry.

FORMULATION OF A WAGE SHARE EQUATION

From the hypotheses outlined above, it is necessary to construct a wage share equation, the two major components being wage rates and labour productivity. The wage share is defined as the proportion of value added that accrues to workers.

While there has been little work carried out on the determinants of the wage share, there has been a good deal of analysis of the determinants of wage rates in the UK. Much of the recent work in the area has been carried out by Stewart (1990 & 1991), assessing the wage differentials of manual workers that are generated by trade unions. In Stewart (1990) this is carried out essentially by deriving wage equations for groups of workers in union and non-union plants from the Workplace Industrial Relations Survey data. Stewart also includes a foreign dummy in his wage in his work, which tends to be insignificant, in contrast to the work carried out by Blanchflower (1986) for example, who determines that there is indeed a foreign mark-up. In these studies, the major determinants of variation in wage rates are skill levels, unionisation, and the age of the plant. Plant age is an important factor, due to the nature of the variables involved. It is generally the older plants that still operate the classification system of skilled, semi-skilled and unskilled manual jobs, and it is these types of plants with more traditional bargaining methods where workers' bargaining power is strongest. This is of course in addition to the obvious human capital explanations of why skilled workers are paid higher wages.

A wage share equation is estimated using a 'logit transformation' of the dependent variable. This will of course test the first hypothesis, that labour productivity is indeed the major determinant of the wage share. The formulation of the wage share equation is as follows:

$$\text{WAGESHARE} = a + \beta_1 * \text{PROD} + \beta_2 * \text{AGE} + \beta_3 * \text{SKILL} + \beta_4 * \text{UNION} + \beta_5 * \text{UNSKILL} + \beta_6 * \text{INTERN} + \beta_7 * \text{MANPAY} + \beta_8 * \text{FOREIGN} + \text{Industry dummies}[1] + e \qquad (4.1)$$

From what has been said above, the predicted signs of the coefficients are as follows:

$$\beta_1 < 0, \beta_2 > 0, \beta_3 > 0, \beta_4 > 0, \beta_5 < 0, \beta_6 > 0, \beta_7 > 0, \beta_8 < 0.$$

The major determinants are expected to be labour productivity and wage rates. One would expect a positive significant coefficient on the age variable here, which would act as a supplement to the union coverage variable. The relationship between skill levels and the wage share will depend on whether skill levels tend to increase productivity to a

---

[1] See Appendix for further discussion.

greater extent than wages. This paper has already demonstrated that in terms of the foreign firms' wage differentials do not match the productivity advantages, so it is likely that plants with high proportions of skilled workers have a lower wage share due to the productivity gains. As has been shown, the relationship between wages and productivity is not as close as may be imagined. In terms of the ability of high productivity firms to generate a surplus over wages, it could therefore even be the case that plants with a high proportion of skilled manual workers will be able to gain more in terms of productivity, than they have to pay in terms of higher wages. The INTERN variable is also included as an indicator of bargaining power, as is outlined above, this is an important factor when assessing the relationship between wages and productivity. The data that are used here also includes all the foreign-owned manufacturing plants in the sample, such that one can test the extent to which the foreign-owned firms, despite their higher wage rates, are able to maintain a lower wage share. In the same way as for wage equations, (see Stewart, 1990 for example) therefore, this model can then be estimated for the whole sample, with a foreign dummy. This enables one to test, not only the first proposition, that labour productivity is indeed the major determinant of the wage share, but also that, the foreign effect in terms of the wage share is negative.

RESULTS

The results for equation 4.1 are given in Table 4.2.

The two major determinants of variations in the wage share are, as expected, the productivity and pay variables. These results illustrate that the model does work as outlined in the hypotheses, with the extremely high 't' value on the productivity coefficient suggesting that the major determinant of a low wage share is likely to be high productivity rather than low wages. However, it is interesting that, despite having the appropriate signs, the human capital variables are insignificant, as is the vertical integration variable. There is evidence that union coverage may not be an appropriate indicator of union activity, particularly for new plants with single-union deals. The older plants are those characterised by collective bargaining, and demarcation regulations that are seen as detrimental to productivity. In addition to this it is often the case that the wage share rather than wages is bargained over in such circumstances (see for example Deaton and Beaumont, 1980). It is also interesting to note that the skill variables work in the way suggested, although the effect is

Table 4.2   The Estimation of the Equation for the
Whole Sample.
Dependent Variable Wage Share.

Variable	Coefficient	't' value
Constant	0.8	8.21**
PROD	$-5.7.10^{-5}$	-21.23**
UNION	$-3.2.10^{-3}$	-0.007
SKILL	-0.07	-0.72
UNSKILL	0.02	0.22
AGE	0.0035	2.56**
INTERN	0.07	1.23
MANPAY	0.20	7.40**
FOREIGN	-0.065	-2.25**
METAL^2	0.29	3.41**

Mean of dependent variable: 0.87.
$R^2 = 0.57$ F(14, 406) = 39.18**.
Log L = -189.186 SSR = 60.18.

weak. The other major result from this model concerns the coefficient on the foreign ownership variable, indicating that indeed FOEs have a lower wage share (and therefore greater profitability) than the DOEs.

We now come to the analysis for the DOE sample. The equation to be estimated here is as follows.

$$\text{WAGESHARE} = a + \beta_1 * \text{PROD} + \beta_2 * \text{AGE} + \beta_3 * \text{SKILL} + \beta_4 * \text{UNION} + \beta_5 * \text{UNSKILL} + \beta_6 * \text{INTERN} + \beta_7 * \text{MANPAY} + \beta_8 * \text{FORSHARE} + \text{Industry dummies} + e \tag{4.2}$$

What is therefore being tested here is the effect that a significant foreign presence has on the domestic sector. For the wage share to fall due to a foreign presence, a situation must develop where the general wage rate is bid up significantly, without any productivity gain. This is why it is appropriate to include the foreign share in an industry rather than, say the average wage paid by the foreign sector. As has already been demonstrated, foreign firms do pay higher wages than DOEs, but

---

[2] The only industry dummy that is reported here out of the six used is the one for the metal works industry, as that is the only one which is even approaching significance.

Table 4.3 Equation Estimated for the UK owned
Sample, Including the Foreign Share Variable.
Dependent Variable, Wage Share.

Variable	Coefficient	't' value
Constant	0.76	6.38**
PROD	$-5.8.10^{-5}$	-18.64**
UNION	$-6.9.10^{-2}$	-0.97
SKILL	-0.09	-0.08
UNSKILL	0.05	0.54
AGE	0.0026	2.01**
INTERN	0.03	0.41
MANPAY	0.20	6.59**
FORSHARE	0.72	3.11**
CHEMICAL	-0.21	-1.92*
METAL	0.26	2.61**

Mean of dependent variable: 0.90.
$R^2 = 0.56$ $F(14, 334) = 30.51$** Log L $= -168.63$ SSR
$= 53.71$.

the impact of this will clearly depend on the size of the foreign sector at the industry level. Thus, for the third hypothesis to hold, one would expect the coefficient on the foreign share variable to be positive. The results from estimating equation 2 are given in Table 4.3.

The most striking result here is the coefficient on the foreign share variable. This signifies that a foreign presence does tend to push wages up throughout the industry, with the result that the wage share is bid up in the UK sector. This is even more striking when one considers that the distribution of FOEs in the UK is skewed towards the high productivity industries. Therefore despite the fact that there is an inverse correlation between the foreign share in an industry and the wage share, the out-lined effect is shown up clearly, such that the third proposition is accepted.

Apart from the above result, and the fact that as already explained the wage share in the UK sector is slightly higher than for the whole sample, many of the variables work in exactly the same way as discussed above. It is however clear from these results that the presence of foreign competitors does cause an increase in the general wage share in the industry. Thus while the wage differential is nowhere near as great as the productivity differential, it nevertheless causes a general bidding up of DOE wage shares, with the obvious implications for the profitability of the UK manufacturing.

THE AGE EFFECT AND BARGAINING STRUCTURES

This discussion has also touched on the 'age' effect of respective plants, and tried to allow for differences caused by this rather than by the so-called 'foreign' effect. Indeed, for plants that have been in operation for less than ten years, there is a distinct pattern to the nature of the foreign-owned firms. Labour productivity is well above the average for the foreign-owned sector, at £16521 p.a., while mean wages are below average, £3.35 per hour, and a wage share value of 0.55. These plants match very well to the established view of new foreign-owned capacity in the UK, in that many have 100% union coverage and collective bargaining agreements, but also list only one union as party to the bargaining mechanism. The single-union deals appear to be with either the Transport and General Workers Union (TGWU), or the Amalgamated Engineering Union (AEU), rather than the electricians union, the EETPU, who, although they have members in at least two of these plants, are not recognised for bargaining purposes by any of the firms. The percentage of skilled workers in the plant is also very low at 9.6%, around half the sample average. This contrasts with the old foreign-owned plants, that have higher wages, although still below average, £3.65, and lower labour productivity, £11984 p.a. and a mean wage share of 0.82. Less have structured pay negotiation, with many plants not recognising a union at all. While the new foreign-owned ones are concentrated in the North and North West, the older plants appear to be located around the more prosperous areas of the UK such as the South East with also a high proportion in the East Midlands.

From what is said above, there may be differences in the structure of bargaining within the two samples, or differences in the general model between the two sets of firms. Using a sub-sample of all those firms that have 100% union coverage (although not necessarily through one trade union), it is possible to demonstrate the pure foreign effect. Although the mean wages of the foreign and UK-owned samples are £3.54 and £3.71 per hour respectively, a test of differences in structure between the two samples, using the F-statistic fails using this data. Comparing the two sub-samples where unions are not present, reveals an almost uni-causal model in the case of the UK-owned sample, where labour productivity determines wages.

Thus, while the relationship between wage rates and labour productivity may be more complex in the foreign-owned sample, productivity is still the most important determinant of wages, and indeed there is evidence that the presence of the more efficient foreign-owned firms does cause the wage share to increase throughout the industry, without improving average productivity. This may be due to the fact that their presence increases the demand for skilled labour, enhancing the industry-level bargaining position of unions, while it is those very firms that are in many ways in the most favourable bargaining position in the industry. This, together with the significant AGE variable in the wage share equation (it is in the older plants where the unions' position is most established) suggests that while wages follow labour productivity. It may be the wage share that is bargained over, implicitly or otherwise, something that is consistent with many theoretical bargaining models. This however is a question that is addressed elsewhere.

CONCLUSIONS

From the results presented above, it is clear that the most important determinant of the wage share in UK industry, both in terms of FOEs and domestic firms is labour productivity. There is also clearly a significant negative foreign effect in terms of explaining the wage share (see table 1), which is due to the variation in pay and productivity between the samples. In addition to this, the foreign sector does pay higher wages, such that the second hypothesis holds, as does the third. The presence of FOEs does cause a bidding up of wages in DOEs, such that these firms experience a profit squeeze through an increased wage share.

It may well be argued that all the results presented here are what would be expected of a free market economy, with the most efficient and technologically advanced firms becoming the most successful. However, free market economics would also predict that those DOEs that stay in existence would be those who would make productivity gains. There are indeed numerous theoretical reasons why such 'catching up' should occur between the domestic and foreign sectors, the most plausible being technology transfer, see Cantwell (1989). There is, however, no reason to suppose that these productivity gains can be made by the DOEs in the same time scale as they have to pay wage increases. The only alternative is the type of productivity gain that British industry made in the early 1980s, which would be accompanied by large scale factory closures. There is, however, no evidence of productivity gains being made by the DOEs within this framework. This suggests that the second alternative, inward investment resulting in a substitution of employment away from DOEs, is more likely.

It would appear that, for whatever reason, the FOEs are able to generate significant advantage in terms of productivity over the domestic competition and, while inward investment is seen as being a vital constituent of various regional and industrial policies, the wisdom of some of the inward investment incentives must be questioned, particularly those which are available to foreign investors only.

POLICY IMPLICATIONS

The major conclusion from this is that there are serious implications for UK manufacturing, as a result of the large quantities of foreign investment that has occurred in the UK in recent years. It is clear that in addition to the incentives that are in place, further policy actions must be taken. A major aim must be to ensure that the desired technology transfer does occur. If this is achieved, such productivity improvements can only be beneficial to the UK, and indeed may serve to generate employment. Examples here are initiatives such as policies aimed at influencing the sourcing policies of the inward investors, such that the technology is passed on in terms of factors such as quality assurance. An extension of this is the creation of technology networks to ensure that the information flows are optimised. Certainly, however, from these results one must question inward investment incentives that are available while no such policies are in place.

Without initiatives for technology diffusion, the prospects for UK industry are bleak. The incumbent domestic firms suffer from, not only having to compete with firms that ex ante have a productivity advantage, but who's existence reduces still further the profitability of UK manufacturing.

It is certain that productivity gains will have to be made in order to compete effectively, but in the absence of any technological improvements these will be of the type of productivity gains that UK industry made in the early 1980s, either through reductions in output or large scale capital/labour substitution. Either scenario clearly has severe implications for unemployment.

REFERENCES

Blanchflower, D. (1986) Wages and Concentration in British Manufacturing. *Applied Economics* no. 18 pp. 1025–38.

Brush, B.C. and Crane, S.E. (1985) 'Wage share, market power and unionism: Some contrary US evidence.' *The Manchester School*, pp. 417–424.

Cantwell, J.A. (1989) *Technological innovation and multinational corporations*. Oxford: Basil Blackwell.

Cowling, K, and Molho, I. (1980) 'Wage Share, Concentration and Unionism.' *The Manchester School.* pp. 99–115.

Henley, A. (1986) Wage share, concentration and unionism : A reply to Brush and Crane. *The Manchester School.* pp. 104–112.

Kalecki, M. (1971) *Selected Essays on the Dynamics of the Capitalist Economy. 1933–70.* Cambridge University Press.

Stewart, M.B. (1990) Union wage differentials, product market influences and the division of rents. *Economic Journal*, vol. 100. Dec. pp. 1122–1137.

5

Determinants of Respective Bargaining Power Between Workers and Foreign Owned Multinationals in the UK

INTRODUCTION

This chapter analyses some of the previous results in terms of the relative strengths of unions and firms, both strategic and structural, and assesses differences between foreign and domestic firms.

A bargaining model that is applicable to these questions should therefore allow for a measure of bargaining power to be quantified. In this way the results from different samples can be compared. In order to follow this approach, one has to therefore use bargaining power as the exogenous variable, and therefore assume that high wages are evidence of greater bargaining power. This is perfectly consistent with the theory of wages and bargaining, accepting that an important concept in bargaining theory is that the opponent's willingness to concede is as important in determining an individual's bargaining power, as any strategic move that can be made. One can see therefore that the relationship between wages and productivity is consistent with these terms, in that the more successful firms are able to pay more.

The Basic Concepts of a Bargaining Model

A bargaining model that illustrates the nature of collective bargaining between a firm and a union is as follows. The model assumes that the firm wishes to employ workers, it has to enter into a bargaining arrangement with the union, and that any workers that are not employed by the firm have the opportunity to receive a "reservation wage", i.e. the best available alternative. This also assumes that there is something to bargain over, that is that by employing some workers at not less than the reservation wage will enable the firm to make a profit. This therefore creates the opportunity for the union to bargain away some of this profit, through a wage above the reservation value by withholding labour. It is also necessary to assume that the firm has some degree of monopoly power in the product market, in order to generate excess profits.

In order for the union to have a significant degree of power, it is necessary to assume that it is costly for the firm to hire non-union labour. In such models, this is often presented through the idea of a pre-entry closed shop, but this need not be the case. There are many institutional reasons why plants are unionised, going back in some cases over seventy years. Obviously where a plant is unionised it would be exceptionally difficult for a firm to circumvent the trade union, for fear of a strike, and as has received a good deal of press coverage, new plants often have 100% union deals in order to provide an established communication structure between the management and the work-force.

One of the most popular formulations of a bargaining model in empirical work is the Efficient Bargaining Model, following McDonald and Solow (1981). The central tenet of these models is that any solution to the problem should be efficient, that is that it maximises the gain to the firm, subject to achieving the given level of gain for the union. It is easy therefore to see that the mathematical formulation of this type of model is a constrained maximisation. All solutions are characterised by the condition that the marginal rate of substitution between wages and employment for the firm is equal to that characterised by the preferences of the trade union.

While the efficient bargaining model does carry many intuitive attractions, in order to gain an insight into absolute levels of bargaining power, an extension of this, in line with the theory of the type derived in a Nash bargaining model, is equally applicable. That is that a maximisation of a combined utility function, such that each party seeks to maximise its gain subject to the actions of the other. This is therefore equivalent to both parties maximising their utilities' subject to the constraints placed by the demands of the other party, rather than the firm maximising it's utility subject to some minimum demand made by the union.

The Nash model is based on the game theory ideas of von Neumann and Morgenstern (1944). In these terms, the bargaining problem is therefore represented as a co-operative non-zero sum game. In this case, while there are obvious gains from trade between firms and workers, the outcome will be determined depending on the respective levels of bargaining power.

Formulating an Estimable Wage Equation

Much of the empirical work that employs a bargaining model is based on the work of De Menil (1971), where a bargaining model is used to formulate a wage equation, which can then be tested empirically. Clearly the way in which the model is formulated will influence the outcome. For example there has been much debate on the nature of trade unions' goals, and how this will affect the determination of the union's utility function.[1]

Traditionally, the objective trade union function has been expressed in terms of the wage rate. Most models will assume that it is this that is bargained over, but given the results of chapter four, the analysis here expresses the union's objective function in terms of the wage bill or the wage share.

Obtaining a Measure of Bargaining Power

One possible method of obtaining bargaining power from wages is presented by Svejnar (1986), using the idea of the joint maximisation of utility functions that is inherent in the Nash model. While it is assumed that, as is outlined in the Nash (1953) model, the two parties make mutual concessions which are induced by their assessment of the relative bargaining strengths, and their fear of disagreement, no attempt to model this specific process is made. However, as is demonstrated below, the measures of risk aversion and bargaining power are important to the analysis.

For the union-firm case, there are clearly only two parties, whose utility functions can be defined as U_1 and U_2, and Svejnar's contribution to the analysis is that the solution to the bargaining problem is defined as m(s), where s is the subset of possible solutions, as:

$$m(s) = \max.\Pi^n_{i=1} U_i{}^{\gamma}i \tag{5.1}$$

The solution maximises the joint utility function, allowing for differences in bargaining power.

(In this case it is assumed that $\gamma_1 + \gamma_2 = 1$.).

---

[1] See for example Dunlop, (1944), or for a more technical treatment, Oswald (1985) or Chapman (1986).

The attractions of this methodology from this point of view are clear. This expressly generates a wage equation that has as parameters the levels of bargaining power of the two parties.

THE MODEL

The purpose of this work, is not to develop a model of union/monopoly bargaining, but to devise a model that will provide an indication of the degree of bargaining power that accrues to the workers' representatives in certain situations. It is therefore necessary to utilise a very general form of the workers' collective utility function, that has some intuitive appeal as well as theoretical basis.

As Svejnar (1986) acknowledges, there are several problems associated with generating a union's utility function by aggregating from what are perceived to be individual preference functions. There is however, considerable evidence to suggest that while it may be wage rates that are the subject of negotiation, both sides are essentially concerned with the wage bill or the wage share.

Thus, assuming risk neutrality in the union, the following union utility function is used:[2]

$$U_w = (WE - W_m E_j) \qquad\qquad (5.2)$$

Where:

W is the average manual wage in the plant.

E is total manual employment.[3]

W_m is the industry average wage.

E_j takes into account differences between the plant and the industry average. Clearly, the industry average employment level is not applicable, due to differences in plant size, so what is used is the following:

$$E_j = SALES_j \times (EMPLOYMENT/SALES)_i \qquad\qquad (5.3)$$

---

[2] The assumption concerning risk neutrality in practice actually derives the result that any difference in the degree of risk aversion between the two parties will alter the estimates of γ, but this is not a significant issue, given what is outlined concerning γ below.
[3] There are four classes of manual workers in WIRS, unskilled, semi-skilled, skilled and foremen, so the value of WE is the total wages that accrue to these groups.

Where $SALES_j$ is the sales of the plant, and $(EMPLOYMENT/SALES)_i$ is the industry average employment/sales ratio for industry i, the plants primary industry, at the four digit level.

Thus, the unions' utility function entails the differential between the revenue that accrues to the workers, and the industry average, corrected for firm size.[4]

This is chosen for several reasons, first of all there is substantial evidence to suggest that unions are concerned with the wage bill rather than with wage rates, and also that many plants take into account agreements that have been reached elsewhere in the industry. Also, it can be seen that a union's aim will be to obtain as large a differential as possible over the market average. It is also worth noting that this allows for more than one union to be involved, and while this may diminish union power, a closed shop is not assumed.

The aim of the firm is to maximise profits, defined as above

$$U_F = \Pi = R - H - WE \qquad (5.4)$$

Where R = revenue, H = overheads.

Many models assume that workers and employers bargain over wages, and employers then determine the level of employment. While this is not wholly realistic, it is nevertheless the case that bargaining is generally over wage rates, with usually some assumptions concerning employment for the coming period.

Estimation of the Bargaining Model

Clearly, the industry average wage Wm is simple to obtain from official sources, but what is somewhat more difficult is the measure for employment on the right hand side of the equation 5. We have a bargaining model here that deals expressly with the wage share rather than simply the wage rate, so it is necessary to allow for some scope in bargaining over employment levels as well as the wage rate.

The regression equation is the one given in equation 5.5, as follows:

---

[4] This does however, produce something that on the face of it may appear to be a strange result, that if labour productivity in the industry declines, then the union's utility falls. The reason for this, is that in the case of E_i/S_i falling, the wage share in the rest of the industry will have increased, so the union at the plant level will seek to catch up.

$$(WE)_k = (W_m E_j)_k + \beta . \Pi_k \quad + e_{1k} \qquad \text{for plant k} \qquad (5.5)$$

With the variables defined as above. Therefore $\beta = \gamma/1 - \gamma$.

Initial Results

The results for the estimation of equation 5.12, with consistent standard errors is as follows:

$\gamma = -0.04853$ standard error $= 0.01649$ 't' value $= -2.94$**

indicating that the degree of bargaining power is significantly negative for the whole sample.[5]

This should not be too surprising, many of the UK firms in the sample pay below average wages for the industry, which is evidence in its self of a lack of union bargaining power.

DETERMINANTS OF BARGAINING POWER

While this model produces good results, and a significant value for the estimate of γ what is important is the way in which this result is interpreted, particularly, in terms of establishing which variables are important in determining bargaining power. There are then two ways that this can be done;

1. Using sub-sets of the data to estimate equation 5.5, and comparing the results.
2. Substituting a vector of variables, $\gamma(Z)$ for the estimate of bargaining power. The reason for the inclusion of many of these variables is clear.[6]

---

[5] It would be surprising in a model such as this if there were not a degree of heteroskedasticity present in the data. The usual range of tests for heteroskedasticity were applied to the results, and while it was not possible to determine the nature of the heteroskedastic disturbances, the more general tests provided evidence, that for the full data set at least, it was not possible to accept the hypothesis of homoskedasticity, and therefore reliable standard errors. For this reason, a routine was used that uses a technique similar to White's (1980) correction method, to generate heteroskedastic-consistent standard errors, and thus allow for valid 't' and F tests.

[6] See appendix 2.

$$WE = W_mE_j + \gamma(Z). \tag{5.6}$$

where $\gamma(Z) =$

$(a_0 + a_1*MANTOT + a_2*STRIKE + a_3*SKILL + a_4*REGUP + a_5 *PLANTNEG + a_6*HORIZ + a_7*NATNEG + a_8*INTERN + a_9*FEMALE + a_{10}*UNION + a_{11}*MARKET) \qquad (5.6a)[7]$

It is often perceived that large plants breed worker alienation and therefore union militancy. The plant size variable is therefore included to take account of this.

The STRIKE variable is included as a measure of union militancy.

The SKILL variable has a positive relationship with wages, but the question remains as to whether the SKILL effect varies to any great extent within the same industry. Only if the percentage of skilled workers in a plant has a significantly positive effect on wage compared with the industry average, will this variable have a positive coefficient in this analysis.

There is no allowance for regional variations captured in the W_mE_j term, so therefore one would expect that the regional unemployment variable will have a negative effect on the degree of union bargaining power, as this may also in part capture any regional differences in wages.

In the area of labour economics, it is often perceived that plant level bargaining is the most effective from the point of view of the union, especially when it is supplementary to a national or industry-wide collective bargaining agreement. One would therefore expect ex ante, the PLANTNEG variable to have a positive coefficient in the equation. Conversely, national bargaining can be in the interest of the firm, as it provides scope for the management to present one policy to the workers, and a lack of flexibility that therefore implies little willingness to bargain away from the stated position. It is therefore possible that the coefficient on the NATNEG variable will be negative. It should be noted however that these variables are not mutually exclusive.

As mentioned above, firms that are vertically integrated may find that they are in a weakened position when negotiating with workers, due to the possibility of a strike interrupting production elsewhere. Thus,

---

[7] What is therefore being presented is a situation where $\gamma(Z)$ is being used as a proxy for $\gamma/(1-\gamma)$, the ratio of union to firm bargaining power, which in this model is clearly the same as a measure of union power.

despite the possibilities for negating this problem, such as holding sufficient stocks to endure the short term, the predicted sign on this variable is positive. Conversely, horizontally integrated firms are able to circumvent industrial action by switching production. Thus, the horizontal variable should have a negative sign.

There are certain industries, such as textiles that are characterised by a high proportion of female workers and low wages. If the phenomenon of women being employed in low paid manual jobs is truly industry-specific, then the FEMALE variable will be insignificant in this equation. However, if the situation is more plant-specific than this, then the sign will be negative.

A high degree of union coverage should automatically increase workers bargaining power, although this may also depend on the degree of militancy of the workers.

The MARKET is a measure of the elasticity of the demand curve that the plant is facing. The sign on this variable should be negative, as it measures the extent to which the firm is able to pass on any cost increase to the consumer. The more elastic the demand function, the less likely the firm is to concede to a wage demand, and as an important part of any bargaining model is the likelihood for one side to concede, the sign on this variable should be significantly negative.

Having outlined the predicted signs on these variables, the actual results for the foreign sample are given below:

Table 5.1   The Determinants of Bargaining Power.

Variable	Coefficient	't' value
MANTOT	$-2.42.10^{-6}$	-0.22
STRIKE	$1.8.10^{-3}$	0.34
REGUP	-0.014	-0.05
PLANTNEG	$-1.78.10^{-3}$	-0.09
SKILL	-0.107	-0.144
NATNEG	-0.046	$-2.74**$
INTERN	0.094	$7.09**$
HORIZ	$-3.6.10^{-2}$	$-2.35**$
FEMALE	0.013	0.15
UNION	$9.5.10^{-4}$	$2.44**$
MARKET	-0.45	$-2.36**$

number of observations = 72. $R^2 = 0.99$. F = 15.47**.
** significant at the 5% level.
*significant at the 10% level.

With the exception of the coefficient on the plant size variable, which is insignificant, most of the variables act in the predicted direction. Clearly the structure of the firm is well known to the union, who understand when this puts the workers in a strong position. The most likey example of this is where the firm is vertically integrated. Equally, employees bargaining power is reduced through horizontal integration. The MARKET variable is in a sense a good indication of the management's willingness to agree to certain pay claims, as the variable measures the firm's perception of the elasticity of its market demand curve. This concurs with the results discussed by Dowrick (1989) and Stewart (1990), that power in the product market is one of the most important determinants of the extent to which firms are likely to concede to union wage demands. It is interesting that the local unemployment level would appear to have little relevance in bargaining situations, which is an interesting and somewhat surprising result, given the perception of foreign firms moving into the depressed regions of the UK, in order to exploit the large available labour force. This again provides a striking contrast between the coverage of foreign firms in the media, being perceived as the new Japanese owned operations, and the bulk of the MNEs in the UK that are the well established US firms. The STRIKE variable in the case of the foreign-owned operations would appear to have little effect on way or the other.

The other interesting result that shows up here is the contrast between the apparent effectiveness of national and plant-level bargaining. It has often been suggested that, while national bargaining is the most widespread, where it exists this is very much an industry-wide phenomenon, and it is then those workers that have additional local deals that will gain the most. This, however, would seem to be disproved for the foreign sample as a whole, in that plant level bargaining has little effect on the outcome, and that the influence of national bargaining is detrimental to the union. However, it is also likely to be the case that where firms are dealing with more than one trade union, the firm's degree of co-ordination at the national, or even international level is going to be greater than of the workers. Also, where, in the limit the multinational has the ability to make the threat that it can leave the UK completely, any amount of union co-ordination within the UK can be offset by the firm. It is also interesting SKILL has little effect in the model, while unionisation does, as the maintenance of differentials is one of the foremost aims of most trade unions. That the FEMALE variable has no significant sign may well be due to the fact that the employment of women operatives in

Table 5.2 The UK-owned Sample.

Variable	Coefficient	't' value
MANTOT	$2.42.10^{-5}$	4.64**
STRIKE	0.004	−4.72**
REGUP	−0.32	−1.97*
PLANTNEG	$8.0.10^{-3}$	−0.9
SKILL	0.58	3.10**
NATNEG	0.0033	−3.81**
INTERN	$1.3.10^{-4}$	0.09
HORIZ	−0.0332	−0.37
FEMALE	0.041	−2.67**
UNION	$2.3.10^{-4}$	1.94*
MARKET	−0.063	1.19

number of observations 349, $R^2 = 0.98$ F = 17.42**.
** significant at the 5% level.
* significant at the 10% level.

foreign-owned plants is very much in line with inter-industry variations, and therefore does not cause any deviation from the industry average.

The estimation of this equation for the UK-owned plants however, produces some different results, illustrated in Table 5.2.

It would appear from these results that domestic plants are not as effective at preventing large plants breeding worker alienation and union militancy, and indeed the results for the domestic sector are much more in line with what would be predicted by the theory of bargaining power. National level collective bargaining appears to be in the workers' interest, while the effect of local unemployment would appear to be greater in the UK-owned plants. It is also noticeable that the skill variable and the percentage of female workers are significant and have the predicted sign.

The one major exception to these coefficients estimating as predicted is the one on the STRIKE variable. One would imagine that a union that could call its members out on strike would have increased bargaining power, rather than less. However, one can imagine that, due to the way the model is formulated, it is those workers that perceive their standard of living to have been eroded, and would therefore show up in the analysis as having a low level of bargaining power, that would be willing to forgo earnings in order to gain an increase. In other words the cause of a strike can be frustration on the part of the workers rather than as show of union militancy, that strikes are used as a last resort by workers who perceive that they have the least to lose.

It is worth noting here that the R^2 is slightly improved by this formulation of the model over equation 5, and that its corresponding version out-performs 5a. There has been no work carried out on a possible functional form, but this linear form has a high level of explanatory power, and gives clear results. It is worth noting here that, while bargaining power is a concept applied to situations involving one employer and one union, the measure derived thus far pertains to the workers in general, including plants without union representation. This could well account for the estimate of γ in this equation. The final variable that is significant in this case is FEMALE. It is often construed that the proportion of manual workers that are female is an inter industry rather intra industry phenomenon, with certain sectors employing a high ratio of women to men, the usually cited example being textiles. If this were the case then one would expect this idea to be caught by the $W_m E_j$ term, and then any FEMALE term in the second part of the equation to be insignificant. That this is not the case demonstrates that indeed even within these sectors bargaining union power is reduced with any increase in the percentage of women employed, as in sectors not known for employing large numbers of women on the shop floor. This result may again change when one looks at the highly unionised plants only, as high a level of female employment is often synonymous with a low level of union recognition. The other significant variable is the market power measure. It is important, as that workers' bargaining power is dependent as much on the extent to which the firm is likely to concede, as it is in any positive moves that the union can make. This result is, therefore, an indication that the greater the capacity the firm has for passing its cost increases onto its customers, the more likely it is to concede. Finally, the two variables that appear to have little effect on the levels of bargaining power are the measures of horizontal and vertical integration, but the inclusion of these is more pertinent to the foreign-owned sector, and the study of the bargaining power that it generates specifically for MNEs as opposed to domestic firms.

Again, the union coverage variable is significant, while the STRIKE variable is not, which again has implications for future research when wishing to proxy union militancy or activity.

The only surprising result here is the significant negative coefficient on the national bargaining variable. In the case of the UK-owned plants, as is traditionally the line in the literature, it is perceived that a national bargaining structure will be an aid to the unions; as they can use the collective bargaining to their advantage through combined strength.

Further Investigation

The results from the estimation of equation 5.12a have suggested at some of the possible reasons for the degree of union bargaining power varying across firms, but it is also possible to obtain an estimate of γ for firms displaying certain characteristics. What is important here is the difference from the result for γ using the full data set, i.e. the estimate of γ for either the complete UK or foreign-owned sample. Table 5.3 illustrates these differences.

Table 5.3 provides a summary of the estimates of γ for various subsamples of the data.

This illustrates some of the causes in differences in bargaining power, and provides not only a contrast between the foreign and domestic sector, but also the different reasons for unions and firms to experience different levels of bargaining power, both through strategic moves, such as the creation of a national bargaining framework, or the degree of unionisation, and those that derive from the general firm strategy, such as the degree of vertical or horizontal integration, and finally those that are exogenous factors, such as the firm's degree of monopoly power in the product market.

These calculations also provide a good illustration of something mentioned several times here, following Enderwick (1985), that the extent of vertical integration within an MNE will enhance significantly the degree of union power at a particular site.

A result that contradicts several previous opinions of the behaviour of multinationals in host countries is the estimate of γ from the sample of plants in areas of high unemployment. In contrast to the workers in UK firms, whose degree of bargaining power diminishes as unemployment, there is no evidence of this within the foreign-owned sector. Finally, there is the replication of a result from chapter four, that in cases where increased costs cannot be passed on to the consumer, a foreign firm is more likely to resist a wage claim than is a UK-owned plant. Given the previous results, it is not surprising that the workers' situation would appear to be severely damaged by a lack of union representation, particularly when dealing with a multinational. The diminished level of bargaining power that workers are able to generate in this position is a significant result. Given the formulation of this model, bargaining power is seen to be demonstrated by the deviation in the wage bill from the weighted (by size) industry average. Therefore, inter-industry differences will not show up. It is possible to demonstrate from these results, that unions are able to advance the position of their members, or at least

Table 5.3 Summary of Estimates of γ for Various Sub-Samples of the Data.

Nature of Sample	Foreign-Owned Plants Est' of γ	No of obs	UK-Owned Plants Est of γ	No of obs
Full Sample	0.019 (0.0057)	72	−0.051 (0.015)	349
Horizontally integrated	0.0094 (0.015)	31	0.0029*+ (0.01)	111
Vertically Integrated	0.073*+ (0.0096)	27	0.0039 (0.065)	36
Unionised	0.025 (0.017)	58	−0.05 (0.016)	336
Non-union	0.0017*− (0.0024)	12	−0.064 (−0.064)	65
Market = 0	0.024 (0.014)	39	−0.062 (0.012)	175
Market > 10%	−0.011*− (0.0075)	15	−0.018 (0.018)	94
high REGUP	0.043*− (0.0095)	37	−0.056 (0.014)	190
low REGUP	0.057 (0.018)	35	−0.011 (0.017)	159
national bargaining	0.023 (0.0066)	51	−0.0099*+ (0.013)	255
no national bargaining	0.012 (0.0095)	21	−0.0727*− (0.0044)	94
High profit	0.021 (0.02)	25	−0.054 (0.014)	105
Low profit	0.055 (0.023)	37	0.031*+ (0.039)	152
N. American	0.0488*+ (0.0077)	47		
European	−0.0043*− (0.0747)	21		

standard errors in parenthess.
*+ significantly greater than 0.019.   *+ significantly greater than −0.051.
*− significantly less than 0.019.   *− significantly less than −0.051.

workers are in a far worse position in dealing with foreign-owned firms if they are not represented.

In order to obtain more specific results of the differences in bargaining power that are generated by varying plant-level characteristics, it is possible to carry out a Chow type test on the residuals from the estimates of equation 5. This is then a test of whether the overall model performs as

Table 5.4   The Sub-Samples Compared.

Sub-samples compared	F_O	Combined sample size
All Foreign/Domestic Firms	15.51**	421
All Vertically integrated	9.85**	53
All Horizontally integrated	0.078	142
All nationally negotiated	3.36**	306
All unionised plants	13.11**	336
Non-union plants	3.17**	69
All with low market power	0.043	109
All with high market power	11.19**	214
All with high local unemployment	9.06**	227
All with low local unemployment	0.82	193

well for the combined sample, as it does for each of the sub-samples separately, which in the case of this single variable model is equivalent to testing whether the estimates of γ from the two sub-samples are equal. There are several obvious possibilities for inter-sample differences, with the results given in Table 5.4.

Many of these F tests produce highly significant results, as would be expected, however these results are as important for those F values that are not significant, as for those that are. While MNEs are able to generate an advantageous position for themselves in the absence of trade unions, there is little evidence that workers are exploited where this is possible. For example, where the MNE is horizontally integrated, while it may well derive a better bargaining position than if it were internationally vertically integrated, the firm does no better than if it were a national firm. There are two reasons for this, firstly a uni-national firm with a horizontally integrated structure will often be faced by national bargaining, which is in the union's interest, thus increasing the estimate of γ for the UK sample. It may also be, however, that the unions will be aware of the multinationals position, and therefore be less willing to concede for fear of being exploited. This would also appear to be the case where the MNE has a plant in an area of high unemployment. There has been a good deal of media attention directed towards such plants in recent times, but there is little evidence, either that MNEs are heavily concentrated in these regions, or that they are able to derive extra bargaining power from such a position.

Equally as important in this part of the analysis are the comparisons between various sections of the foreign sub-sample. The foreign sample comparisons are given in Table 5.5.

Table 5.5   Foreign Sub-Samples Compared.

Sub-samples	Fo	Combined sample size
Vertically/Horizontally integrated	5.52**	48
Nationality (N.America, Europe, RoW)	19.24**	72
Location within the UK, by ten regions	2.05**	72
National Agreement/ No National Agreement	0.462	72

These results are again are much as expected, to derive such a strong result when comparing the firms with differing structures, with only 48 observations, is an indication that this difference is exceptionally marked in this sample. Despite the advantage that an MNE can generate through national bargaining in the host country, this does not demonstrate a strong difference in outcomes between the two groups. What one can say however, is that it would seem that the advantage in national bargaining would appear to lie with the firm in the case of a multinational, and the union in the case of the domestic firm, hence the difference when comparing the foreign and domestic sectors, but no difference in the intra-foreign sector analysis.

UNION – MULTINATIONAL BARGAINING

Outlined thus far are some results that give a general indication of the variables that effect the levels of bargaining power in a general sense. However, what is equally important in this analysis, is the extent to which this is affected by the strategic moves that may be made in the context of a single union – multinational bargaining situation. In order to do this, a sub-sample of the foreign-owned plants is used, where union coverage is over 80% with one union representing at least half the workers. This then assumes a significant degree of union power, without restricting the sample to a set of single union deal situations. It is therefore inherent in this model that several of the exogenous variables will be the result of previous moves by one of the parties, for example to form a certain bargaining framework, or develop pay structures to protect the differentials of skilled workers. It is conceivable that the results from this data may be significantly different from the unionised sector of UK-owned plants, given the Chow test results reported above. This would therefore provide a more specific idea of why the bargaining outcomes involving MNEs differ from those involving domestic companies. Due to singularity of data, it is clearly necessary to change the formulation of $\gamma(Z)$ for this model, and therefore this takes the form:

$$\gamma(Z) = a_1{}^*MANTOT + a_2{}^*STRIKE + a_3{}^*REGUP + a_4{}^*SKILL + a_5{}^*SINGLE + a_6{}^*NATNEG + a_7{}^*INTERN + a_8{}^*HORIZ + a_9{}^*FEMRAT + a_{10}{}^*MARKET \tag{5.7}$$

It is assumed that, as all the major unions involved here are recognised for negotiation purposes, there will be some form of plant-level bargaining in each case, so this variable is excluded. However, the SINGLE variable is now included, which is a 'single union agreement' dummy variable. The important ex-ante issue here, is whether any of the union power variables have a positive effect in this case, and whether the effects of any of the structural variables, now that a certain degree of union power is assumed.

The results for the foreign-owned sector are then as given in Table 5.6.

Again we see that strikes are the actions of the most disadvantaged workers in this model, while unions do work to protect the differentials of skilled workers through their increased bargaining power. The explanation of this heavy negative coefficient on the STRIKE variable could

Table 5.6   Determinants of Bargaining Power in the Foreign-owned Sector.

Variable	Coefficient	't' value
MANTOT	$-3.07.10^{-6}$	-0.27
STRIKE	-0.23	$-16.24{**}$
REGUP	0.25	0.86
SINGLE	-0.068	$-1.76{*}$
SKILL	0.0651	$2.03{**}$
NATNEG	-0.045	$-4.23{**}$
INTERN	0.106	$9.54{**}$
HORIZ	-0.048	$-3.83{**}$
FEMALE	0.033	0.43
MARKET	-0.41	$-2.62{**}$

number of observations = 58. R^2 = 0.99. F = 15.03**.

well be due to the presence of many agreements between foreign-owned plants and unions, of either an implicit nature, that foreign-owned firms simply pay a premium in order to safeguard industrial peace, or that there is an explicit no-strike single union deal made with a particular union.

Again there is evidence that the MNEs operating in the regions suffering from high unemployment, do not seek to gain significantly from this in terms of the wages paid, and also that in the unionised foreign sector, the female workers do not suffer from an adverse position in terms of bargaining. Given that these women are in generally the highest paid of the manufacturing groups, this is not surprising. In a similar way to the 'national negotiating structure' variable, it is clear that the single union agreements that MNEs have in the UK, are created in the interest of the firm. This result again should not be surprising, as it is clear from many of the plants that have been proposed recently by foreign-owned firms in the UK, the expressed desire for a single union agreement has come from the firm. It is a normal expression in labour economics, that unions seek to attain as much of the surplus accruing from the monopoly power of the firm as possible. We can therefore see that where this monopoly power does not exist, the union's capacity for increasing the rent that accrues to the workers is severely diminished.

These results contrast with those from a similar equation run on the UK-owned sample, which are presented in Table 5.7.

These results, when contrasted with the previous set, make interesting reading, as they demonstrate that there is a more overtly hostile

Table 5.7   Determinants of Bargaining Power in the UK Sample.

Variable	Coefficient	't' value
MANTOT	$2.8.10^{-5}$	4.08**
STRIKE	−0.023	−2.41**
REGUP	−0.29	−2.71**
SINGLE	0.019	1.47
SKILL	0.032	1.21
NATNEG	0.033	1.91*
INTERN	−0.025	−1.56
HORIZ	0.0067	0.37
FEMALE	−0.036	−1.49
MARKET	0.14	0.17

number of observations = 278. R^2 = 0.99. F = 17.00**.

relationship between trade unions and domestic firms, than there is between unions and MNEs in the UK. UK firms have a far greater problem with worker alienation generating union activity, and are more likely to take advantage of high rates of local unemployment to arrive at lower wage settlements than are MNEs. The existence of national bargaining in these cases strengthens the unions' position due the threat of collective action, and the degree of horizontal or vertical integration nationally has little effect.

CONCLUSION

To put this in terms of the Nash bargaining model, the picture is one of a situation where the foreign-owned firms seek to derive a set of bargaining "rules", while at the same time seeking wherever possible to avoid confrontation. This often takes the form of pre-production bargaining, to create agreement on single-union deals and other facets of the bargaining structure before even construction of the plant is commenced. A good example of this was the Ford plant in Dundee, where the firm could not achieve an agreement on its desired form of single union deal, and so decided to locate elsewhere. It would also appear that the foreign firms are better at avoiding confrontation, and are willing to pay higher wages where they realise that it is necessary taking a global view of the company, particularly in the case of vertically integrated structures. This is not to say however that MNEs do not take advantage of the situation when possible, using the threat, implied or open, that in the case of one of several plants at the same stage of the production process, capacity can always be transferred elsewhere. Unions dealing with foreign-owned firms would also appear to be prepared to take a pragmatic approach when seeking wage increases, recognising the possibility of international relocation. It is this capacity to relocate in situations where the profit rate is not acceptable to the parent that creates the bargaining advantage of MNEs, compared with domestic firms. This is demonstrated by the coefficients on the market power variables. A UK firm's lack of market power seems to have little bearing on the outcome, while a foreign firm that cannot pass on its costs does not appear to face the same pressure on wages. This could well be dependent on the internal structure of the MNE. One that allows individual plants a low degree of autonomy, will quickly put pressure on local managers if profits fall, and in such a situation, unions will realise that a profit squeeze through wage pressure can quickly cause closure of the plant through relocation. It is this theme of enhanced firm bargaining power through the internationalisation of production that runs through the whole of this chapter, to the extent that such a phenomenon is significant in determining bargaining power and therefore wage rates. This therefore is an important result in terms of the conclusions of chapter three, that while foreign firms do indeed pay higher wages than UK firms, the foreign/domestic 'wage gap' is not of the same magnitude as the foreign/ domestic productivity differential. Chapter two demonstrates that the 'foreign effect' in UK manufacturing is around 6% in terms of wages, while the productivity differential is substantially larger than this. In terms of the bargaining model, the productivity differential can therefore be seen as an upper limit of the wage differential, and therefore the level of this wage differential, paid by a particular foreign firm over the industry average, is derived from the surplus, which is the subject of the bargaining process. Thus the greater the degree of bargaining power the union has, as determined by these variables, the greater the 'foreign' mark up will be. Thus, the mark up paid by foreign firms is therefore going to vary across industries and firms, as bargaining power varies.

An extension of this is to assess the results in terms of the wage share. As is set out in the previous chapter, the most important variable in terms of the explanation in variation in the wage share across firms, is labour productivity. When this result is allied to the fact that workers in foreign firms are rarely successful in bargaining in attaining more than 50% of the surplus generated by the productivity differential, then one derives the result that, while wages are determined mainly through the bargaining process, the wage share is determined almost solely by labour productivity.

As it is also the case that there is greater variation in labour productivity among the foreign owned firms than for the UK-owned ones, this may be an explanation of the greater variation in the wage share within the foreign-owned sector.

This analysis ties in well with the results concerning the relationships between wage rates and labour productivity in the two sectors, as given in chapter 3. The weakness in the relationship between productivity and wages in foreign firms may be due to this bargaining explanation of wage rates. The 'going rate' idea comes in here, because what we are analysing is the distribution of the foreign productivity surplus, such that foreign firms will pay the industry average plus a mark-up, in other words a rate that is akin to the industry average, plus a bargaining-dependent proportion of their productivity advantage.

This would also account for the greater variation in wage share that exists among foreign firms, as it is also the case that the foreign sector has a greater variation in productivity, despite the distribution of foreign firms being skewed towards the high-wage high productivity sector.

REFERENCES

de Menil, G. (1971) *Bargaining: Monopoly power versus union power*. Cambridge, Mass: MIT Press.
Dowrick, S. (1989) Union – oligopoly bargaining. *Economic Journal*. no. 99 December pp. 1123–1142.
Enderwick, P. (1985) *Multinational Business and Labour*. London Croom-Helm.
McDonald, I.M. and Solow, R.M. (1981) Wage Bargaining and Employment. *American Economic Review*. vol. 71 pp. 898–908.
Stewart, M.B. (1990) Union wage differentials, product market influences and the division of rents. *Economic Journal*, vol. 100. Dec. pp. 1122 – 1137.
Nash, J. (1953) Two-person cooperative games. *Econometrica*, 21. pp. 128–40.
Svejnar, J. (1986) Bargaining Power, Fear of Disagreement and Wage Settlements: Theory and Evidence from US Industry. *Econometrica*, vol. 54 no. 5, pp. 1055–78.
von Neuman, J. and Morgenstern, O. (1944) *Theory of Games and Economic Behaviour*. Princeton University Press. Princeton, New Jersey.

6

The Dynamic Analysis

ISSUES RAISED IN THE CROSS SECTIONAL STUDY

Thus far, all the analysis has been in terms of cross section studies using either plant level or industry level data. This chapter is concerned with some analysis of the changes in wages, productivity and employment. This is an assessment of the domestic and foreign-owned sector of UK manufacturing between 1983 and 1986. Despite the fact that this does not involve a great time span, it is still possible to generate some interesting results here, particularly when one considers the previous three chapters.

For example, in chapters three and four the fact that a foreign presence in an industry can cause wages to be increased in the domestic sector is presented. However, using cross- sectional data it is difficult to differentiate between this effect and the distribution effect of chapter two. Indeed, the whole of the previous chapter is devoted to a bargaining model explains a good deal of inter-plant and inter industry wage differences. However, as in practice collective bargaining is essentially addressed at changes in rates of pay (i.e. wage increases), at least some attention should be paid to this.

Finally, little attention has been paid to the employment effects of the foreign-owned manufacturing sector in the UK. Employment in manufacturing fell steadily throughout the 1970s (see diagram 2.5), and therefore it is necessary to address the issue of whether the foreign-owned plants fared better than domestic industry. Chapter three demonstrates the inherent productivity advantage that these plants have. It is therefore necessary to derive a measure for this comparative advantage, in addition to an assessment of the sectoral differences in performance. The most applicable measure of competitive advantage, particularly when assessing a firms' success in terms of its labour market policies, is that of unit labour costs.

Fagerberg (1988) uses this approach in a six equation simultaneous model incorporating explanations of economic growth, the trade balance, terms of trade, growth of exports, growth of imports and investment. Relative unit labour costs are included in the explanations of terms of trade, imports and exports and are significant in each case. The Fagerberg model clearly requires re-defining in order to be applicable to the firm or industry level. Unit labour costs, together with the various other factors discussed in previous chapters, could well be important in determining firm growth. This is important in order to assess the dynamic effects on both wages and employment of foreign firms in UK manufacturing. It is necessary to assess the extent to which their performance differs from the UK average, and also to explain some of the wage and employment differences. This also ties in with some of the issues outlined in chapter one, concerning the 'level' of production in which the firm is engaged. For example, it is likely that those plants that have a high degree of research and development linked to production are likely to experience not only more success in terms of productivity, but one would also imagine, of sales. The extent then to which wages follow productivity will then determine the extent to which pay in these firms will increase. It is likely that wages do indeed follow productivity, but with a time lag, such that any productivity gain is not automatically paid out to the employees. In such cases therefore, the high tech plants are likely to have the largest productivity/wage differential.

THE EFFECT OF FOREIGN-OWNED ENTERPRISE ON DOMESTIC WAGES

Chapter four outlines the relationship between the rates of pay in domestic plants, and the size of the foreign-owned sector by employment. The essential conclusion is that there is a bidding up of wages caused by the foreign presence.

Removing any intra-industry effects, it is likely that the relationship between wages and labour productivity, particularly in the foreign-owned sector is likely to be stronger.

It is a common theme in work on wage bargaining that one of the important factors is the degree of market power held by the firm. The less price elastic the firm perceives the demand for its final product to be, the more likely it is to acquiesce to a wage demand, as the firm can pass this cost increase on to the consumer. In the plant level analysis, these elasticities were used directly. At the industry level, such data are not available, so it is necessary to use a measure of concentration, the five firm concentration ratio. Unfortunately however, this is not a particularly good measure of market power for these purposes, and could well explain the insignificant result here. Overall however the wage equation in the model performs well, even without the inclusion of industry dummies, with the foreign share variable behaving as one would expect. The coefficient is significant at the ten per cent level, justifying its inclusion, although we are still unable to determine which of the two effects is stronger.

Explaining Changes in these Variables over Time

The analysis here is at the industry level. The model is then set up in a similar way to the previous analysis, with all the variables being expressed in terms of the changes between 1983 and 1986.

The equation to be estimated for the UK-owned sample is then as follows:

$$PAYi = a_1 + \beta_{11}*PRODi + \beta_{12}*UC + \beta_{13}*SEASTi + \beta_{14}*FEM + \beta_{15}*FORSHARE + \beta_{18}*FORGROW + \beta_{16}*CR5 + \beta_{17}*SIZEi + e_1 \quad (6.1a)$$

$$PRODi = a_2 + \beta_{21}*PAYi + \beta_{22}*INV85 + \beta_{23}*RESEARCH + \beta_{15}*FORSHARE + \beta_{18}*FORGROW + \beta_{16}*CR5 + e_2 \quad (6.1b)$$

In order to test the relationship between the foreign-owned influence in an industry and the rate of pay increases, included in the regression is the level of foreign share by employment in 1986, and the growth in foreign share. A small increase in employment in a foreign-owned sector that is dominated by UK production would show up as an extremely large increase in the foreign share. In addition, these two variables are also included in the productivity equation, in order to determine whether, over time, the presence of foreign-owned firms leads to improved productivity through technological advance. This is one of the major arguments for advocating financial assistance for new foreign-owned plants in the UK.

The results for these equations are then given in Table 6.1.[1]

---

[1] Both dependent variables will always lie between minus one and one, and so a logit transformation was carried out on the dependent variables before using three-stage least squares to estimate the model.

Table 6.1a   The Wage Equation.

Variable	Coefficient	't' value
Constant	-0.18	-1.72*
$PROD_1$	0.48	2.86**
CR5	0.0013	1.92*
SIZE	-0.21	-1.27
FORSHARE	0.29	2.02**
FORGROW	0.06	1.86*
UNION	0.0018	1.39
SEAST	0.001	0.08

Mean of dependant variable = 0.19.
(without logit transformation)
$R^2 = 0.34$. Adjusted $R^2 = 0.27$.

Table 6.1b   The Productivity Equation.

Variable	Coefficient	't' value
Constant	0.31	9.01**
PAY_1	0.38	3.58**
INV85	0.052	3.36**
RESEARCH	0.0009	0.12
FORSHARE	0.061	0.57
FORGROW	-0.011	-0.37

Mean of dependent variable = 0.34.
(without logit transformation)
$R^2 = 0.30$. Adjusted $R^2 = 0.27$.

The mean growth in labour productivity over the period is almost double that of wage growth. It is impossible to determine whether wages do follow productivity, but with a time lag but certainly these results demonstrate that wage and productivity growth are indeed strongly related, with wage growth being significantly lower than productivity growth. It is also noticeable that the increase in value added per employee over the period is approximately double that which would be predicted by inflation alone from 1983 to 1986. Wage increases appear to be on average slightly above the level of inflation, which is what would be expected. This is supported by the coefficient on the labour productivity variable. Less than half of any productivity gain accrues to the workers.

There are several conclusions that can be drawn from these results. Firstly, the fact that the constant in the wage equation is negative suggests that without the existence of bargaining, factors, wages would not have risen even in money terms. Secondly for the first time in this analysis, there is evidence that the existence of market power has a positive influence on wage increases. It is also worth noting that the union power measured by union coverage in this sample has no significant effect. It should be remembered that during this time period, the strengths of unions were constantly being eroded through unemployment and industrial relations laws, so it is not surprising that we find the degree of influence that unions have diminishing.

The two interesting variables are those relating to foreign share. There is a highly significant relationship between the foreign share by employment in an industry, and the rate of growth of wages. This reinforces the claim made in chapter four that the existence of foreign firms does indeed cause a bidding up of wage rates in the domestic sector. In the productivity equation however, there is no similar relationship between foreign share and productivity. It would appear that most of the productivity gains over the period resulting from investment in the capital stock, which is a result one would imagine, or as a result of wage increases. This result is a common theme in these results. Labour productivity is important when explaining wage increases, but also that the reverse is true, that wages appear to exert a positive effect on productivity, the so called human capital approach.

Comparison With the Foreign-Owned Sector

Having determined the effect that the foreign presence in an industry has the effect of causing a wage increase in the UK-owned sector, it is now important to determine the causes of the increase of wages and productivity in the foreign sector. The model is set up in a similar manner, with both foreign share variables included to test whether the presence of other foreign firms causes an increase in wages in the foreign owned plant as it does in a UK-owned one. It is a less likely concept here than in the UK-owned sector, but the idea is worth testing.

In the productivity equation, the investment intensity figure is that for 1986 rather than 1985, as data for the foreign sector for 1985 is not available. Also, the research intensity figure is for the UK as a whole, as a breakdown by nationality of ownership is not available.

Results for the foreign sector are given in Table 6.2.

Table 6.2a   The Wage Equation.

Variable	Coefficient	't' value
Constant	0.02	0.18
PRODi	0.61	7.33**
CR 5	0.004	2.81**
SIZE	−0.06	−1.02
FORSHARE	0.09	0.33
FORGROW	0.02	0.64
UNION	−0.01	−0.52

Mean of dependent variable = 0.24.
(without logit transformation)
$R^2 = 0.66$. Adjusted $R^2 = 0.64$.

Table 6.2b   The Productivity Equation.

Variable	Coefficient	't' value
Constant	0.04	0.98
PAY	0.90	8.20**
INV85	0.04	1.86*
RESEARCH	0.0016	0.1
FORSHARE	0.061	0.57
FORGROW	−0.011	−0.37

Mean of dependent variable = 0.25.
(without logit transformation)
$R^2 = 0.58$. Adjusted $R^2 = 0.56$.

The model for the foreign sector performs better than in the domestic case, with a very strong relationship between wage and productivity growth. This is the converse of the relationship for the plant level data, but the weakness of the relationship at the plant level is due to inter-plant differences, which will not show up in an inter-industry study. There is also evidence that foreign firms pay the highest wages in industries with high levels of industry concentration. This supports the hypothesis that wages increase fastest where costs can be passed on to the consumer. This also concurs with several of the conclusions from chapter five, where collective bargaining is seen as being the way in which a flow of funds is divided between the two parties. Both groups then have a mutual interest in trading, to make these income streams as large as possible. Indeed, this phenomenon has more of an effect on wages than the union coverage variable. Interestingly, the relationship between the foreign share and wages does not exist here, suggesting that the 'bidding up' process is confined to the (lower waged) domestic sector. In the productivity equation, surprisingly there is no relationship between investment intensity and productivity growth, while the human capital argument is even stronger here than in the domestic case. Research intensity again has no effect on productivity gains, which again is surprising. This leads to the conclusion that, particularly in the foreign sector, productivity increases seem to be the result of agreements with the work force concerning the instigation of different working practices, or arrangements involving 'productivity deals'. This often will involve substitutions of capital for labour, but the innovation is carried out overseas. These are the types of agreements that are generally accompanied by pay increases.

Again, another major result here concerns the means of the dependent variables, in the case of the foreign sector, the productivity and wage increases are much closer together than for the domestic sector, where there was a significant difference between them. Productivity growth is greater, but only by 0.7% on average. Indeed, productivity growth outstrips wage growth in the foreign sector in only thirty-three of the fifty-three industries, where this is the case in the domestic sector for all but three industries.

It is also noticeable that the variation in these rates of growth is far greater in the foreign sector than the domestic one, the standard deviations in these growth rates being as follows:

	Pay Increase	Productivity Increase
Domestic Firms	0.06	0.07
Foreign Firms	0.24	0.28

Thus, while the productivity/wage gap is widening in UK manufacturing, the evidence that this is the case in the foreign-owned sector is by no means as conclusive.

The major explanation of this over this time period is, the general economic climate. Employment in manufacturing declined by around 15%, while the nature of the foreign sector changed markedly, with a reduction in US involvement and an increase in new plants owned by Japanese and European companies. New plants operated abroad are notorious for having low levels of value added to begin with, particularly in the case of the Japanese, who tend to commence operations with little more than 'screwdrivering' (see for example Dunning 1986). Thus, the productivity growth experienced by the foreign sector may well have been lower than one would expect, while the corresponding value for the UK sector may have increased for the following reason. During this period the country was experiencing high unemployment and a high rate of factory closures. In such an environment, those firms that go out of business will be those that are the least efficient, and thus, ceteris paribus, the average level of value added per employee is likely to increase.

Although here the model works well, the relationship between wage rates and labour productivity in the foreign owned sector is not as stable as this at the plant level, and that to a degree pay levels are as dependent on the industry averages as plant specific factors. In this case, one could well predict that by the same token, wage increases will depend as much on what is being offered elsewhere as on the success of the particular firm over the period. Thus, in cases where productivity growth has not been high, one would still expect wage growth to occur. It is likely however that workers in industries that experience high rates of productivity growth do experience the highest growth in pay over time.

One possible method of testing this is to carry out a test of structural change in the data, dividing the sample according to the rate of productivity growth. Using the Chow test, one can conclude that, by dividing the sample between those industries that have experienced real productivity growth, and those which have not, there is indeed evidence of a difference in the formulation of wage rate increases over the period. As the most important determinant of wages would appear to be productivity, and given what was said in chapter four concerning this relationship, it is necessary to investigate further the relationship between the wage and productivity variables. A method of testing this would be to formulate the wage equation in the following manner:

$$PAYi = a_1 + \beta_{111}*PRODLOWi + \beta_{112}*PRODHIGHi + \beta_{12}*UC + \beta_{13}*$$
$$SEASTi + \beta_{14}*FEM + \beta_{15}*FORSHARE + \beta_{18}*FORGROW +$$
$$\beta_{16}*CR5 + \beta_{17}*SIZEi + e_1 \qquad (6.3a)$$

Thus, instead of testing for a linear relationship we have the following: Where the foreign sector of a particular industry has experienced real growth in labour productivity over the period, PRODHIGHi takes the value of this growth, and zero elsewhere, and vice versa for the PRODLOWi variable.

Thus, if in terms of wage growth, productivity growth is equally important in all industries, we would expect β_{111} equal to β_{112}. A test of this hypothesis can then be set up.

H_O: β_{111} equal to β_{112}; Those workers in industries with no real increase in labour productivity will become worse off over time, while the extent to which workers in the high productivity sector become better off depends on the actual value of β_{112}.

H_1: β_{111} not equal to β_{112}; The distribution of wage increases relative to productivity gains is not even across all industries.

If β_{111} is greater than β_{112}, then this would imply that the rate of growth of wage rates is more even than the growth of productivity, and thus the wage share is falling in the most successful firms and rising in the low productivity sector. If this is reversed however, then one's conclusion depends on the relative sizes of the wage increases in the two groups. If there is no difference in the workings of the equation for the two groups, then the gap between the rates of pay of manual workers in the two groups will be widening. However, if productivity is insignificant in determining wage increases in the low growth sector, this could well be further evidence of the 'going rate' hypothesis, that wages will have to rise, at least with inflation in order to avoid industrial disputes.

The results from the estimation of equation 6.3a are then given in Table 6.3:

Table 6.3a   The Wage Equation with a Split Productivity Variable.

Variable	Coefficient	't' value
Constant	−0.01	−0.08
PRODLOW	−0.02	−0.10
PRODHIGH	0.59	7.13**
UC	$1.30 . 10^{-2}$	0.80
SEAST	$2.6 . 10^{-3}$	1.45
SIZE	$2.7 . 10^{-2}$	0.59
CR5	$2.22 . 10^{-3}$	2.10**
FORGROW	0.17	3.30**
FORSHARE	0.104	0.52

Mean of the dependent variable = 0.239.
$R^2 = 0.78$.   Adjusted $R^2 = 0.74$.

Clearly, the estimates of the coefficients on the two productivity variables differ markedly, leading one to reject the null hypothesis, and also to conclude that this difference is the major cause of the significant result concerning the Chow test above. Not only do we have a significant difference between the estimates of β_{111} and β_{112}, but also the overall performance of the model has been greatly improved. Also, the FORGROW variable is significant, suggesting that when one allows for this difference in the productivity rates, the degree to which the foreign share has increased will have a significant positive effect on wage growth. Within those sectors in which foreign firms are most successful in terms of growth, the employees are rewarded accordingly.

With this result then, one obviously concludes that the relationship between productivity growth and wage growth only exists in the foreign-owned sector for those industries that have experienced real growth in labour productivity over the period, while it is negligible elsewhere. It should however also be noted that the coefficient on the PRODHIGH variable is estimated to be 0.59, that only 60% of any productivity increase accrues to the workers, so that the productivity/wage gap will be increasing in this sector over time. Indeed, the average rate of productivity growth over the time period is 35% over three years for these industries, while the corresponding figure for wages is 27%. However, the values for the low productivity sector are markedly different. The mean level of productivity growth for the bottom 20 industries in terms of productivity growth is –2%, while wages still grew at an average of 15%, which over the three years is close to the level of inflation, which averaged 4.8% a year.[2] This would suggest therefore that there is indeed a powerful force for wage rates to keep pace with inflation, irrespective of productivity growth. While there is also clear evidence that despite the fact that wages do not rise as fast as productivity, employees of successful firms are rewarded. Thus again, there is the conclusion that those factors that determine wage rates are a combination of the efficiency explanation, the link between wages and productivity, but also several bargaining factors, demonstrating a degree of union power even in situations where productivity is declining in real terms.

EXPLANATIONS OF GROWTH AND EMPLOYMENT

The introduction to this chapter outlines a model that not only assesses the causes of wage and productivity growth, but also attempts to explain changes in employment through the measurement of unit labour costs. This is an adaptation of Fagerberg's (1988) paper concerning international competitiveness, as a five equation simultaneous model incorpo-

---

[2] Source RPI from the CSO data base.

rating the two equations outlined thus far in this chapter. Thus, from this it is possible to develop explanations of not only wages and productivity as defined above, but also sales and employment. This can then be linked with the ideas concerning the technological level of the operation, to determine whether this has implications for employment levels as well as rates of pay. It is suggested for example, by Cowling & Sugden (1987) that due to the higher levels of technology, and a higher capital/labour ratio in the new foreign-owned plants, the levels of employment generated are never as great as may be envisaged. It is therefore possible to test whether foreign firms do indeed substitute capital for labour, or whether the increased investment generates a lower unit labour cost and allows the firm to grow. Of course, for both the foreign and domestic sectors, the major cause of changes in employment levels is likely to be the change in sales over the period, and so in this framework it is necessary to include a sales equation, in an attempt to explain changes in the values of sales over time. This is likely to be more successful for the domestic sector than for the foreign firms, due to the fact that there may be some change due to decisions taken on a global scale for firms to enter or leave particular markets, while UK based firms are more likely to remain concentrated in the UK business. The major cause of changes in sales over time at the industry level is likely to be the general economic climate, but of course changes in aggregate demand are likely to affect some sectors of the economy more than others. For this reason, a series of industry dummy variables is included in the sales equation, as an attempt to allow for these sectoral differences in cyclical demand.

The remaining three equations are formulated as follows:

$$\text{ULC86} = a_3 + \beta_{31}*\text{PROD} + \beta_{32}*\text{CR5} + \beta_{33}*\text{INV} + \beta_{34}*\text{PAY} + \beta_{35}*\text{RESEARCH} + e_3 \qquad (6.1c)$$

$$\text{EMPLOYi} = a_4 + \beta_{41}*\text{SALESi} + \beta_{42}*\text{ULCi} + \beta_{43}*\text{INV85} + \beta_{44}*\text{RESEARCH} + \beta_{45}*\text{UNION} + \beta_{36} + e_4 \qquad (6.1d)$$

$$\text{SALESi} = a_5 + \beta_{51}*\text{ULCi} + \beta_{52}*\text{CR5} + \beta_{53}*\text{INV85} + \beta_{54}*\text{RESEARCH} + (\text{Industry dummies}) + e_5 \qquad (6.1e)$$

Many of these variables, including all the explanatory variables in equation 6.3 are defined above, ULC86 is the unit labour costs for the relevant industry and sector in 1986, measured as:

direct labour costs/total sales.

Productivity, research and development, and investment are expected to have a negative effect on unit labour costs, by reducing costs and possibly causing a capital/labour substitution through technical change. The five firm concentration ratio is also expected to have a negative effect on unit labour costs through a positive effect on the price – cost margin, and the coefficient on the pay variable is expected to be positive.

Equation 6.4 estimates the effects that different variables will have on EMPLOYi, the proportional change in manual employment between 1983 and 1986. The most obvious cause of changes in the levels of employment is a change in sales of the industry, measured by SALESi, the coefficient on which is expected to be positive. The change in industry unit labour costs (ULCi) is expected to have a positive coefficient in the employment equation. An increase in unit labour costs will accompany an expansion of employment, (this shows the importance of estimating these in the three equation system, as one would certainly expect unit labour costs to be inversely related to sales). The intensity of investment will have the opposite effect by signalling a capital/labour substitution by the firm. Outlined elsewhere is the likelihood of unions seeking to bargain not only over wages but also in terms of manning levels, so the unionisation variable is included here.

Estimating the determinants of changes in sales, particularly for the foreign, is likely to be difficult, but the main thrust of the argument here is that one would expect unit labour costs to have a significantly negative relationship with the change in sales. Those industries that are best able to compete are able to grow the fastest, much as in Fagerberg's (1988) analysis where low relative unit labour costs are determined to be one of the major sources of economic growth.

The purpose of this model is to determine, firstly whether the foreign sector does indeed have the competitive advantage in terms of unit labour costs, and then secondly how this advantage may be explained. The extent to which this advantage then generates growth in terms of employment through sales growth can also be tested.

This model may be presented in terms of a five equation system, including the determinants of wage and productivity growth. However, when estimated, none of the parameters are dependent on the first two equations being estimated within the system, so it is therefore appropriate to remove and estimate the wage and productivity growth equations separately.

The results of estimating this system for the two sectors of the economy are as follows:

Table 6.1c   Dependent Variable ULC86.

Variable	Coefficient	't' value
Constant	0.212	5.15**
PROD	$-9.12.10^{-6}$	-7.67**
CR5	$-6.7.10^{-5}$	-0.16
INV85	-0.016	-1.65*
RESEARCH	$0.93.10^{-2}$	2.19**
PAY	$1.77.10^{-5}$	3.16**

Mean of the dependent variable = 0.202.
$R^2 = 0.59$.   Adjusted $R^2 = 0.54$.

The one exception to the predictions made above is the positive significant relationship at the industry level of research intensity with unit labour costs. It is not immediately obvious why this should be the case. The only explanation is that the research carried out is in terms of new products that require more skilled labour to produce them, thus increasing the proportion of the value added that is paid in wages. Research and development that is carried out with a view to making the production process more efficient is likely to increase labour productivity, and then possibly wages, but at the expense of employment. All the other variables have the expected signs, although the concentration ratio is insignificant. This again may be a result of it being an imperfect measure of market power.

Table 6.1d   Dependent Variable EMPLOYi.

Variable	Coefficient	't' value
Constant	-0.29	-5.81**
SALESi	1.52	7.74**
ULCi	0.53	7.44**
INV85	-0.015	-0.58
RESEARCH	-0.019	-1.32
UNION	$-0.9.10^{-3}$	-0.59

Mean of the dependent variable = -0.078.
$R^2 = 0.58$.   Adjusted $R^2 = 0.55$.

As expected, positive unit labour cost changes and sales increases have a positive effect on industry level employment, with investment and Research and development having negative if insignificant coefficients. These results also demonstrate that supposed high levels of union power were unable to resist job cutbacks, and the average reduction in industry employment of manual workers was 7.8% over the period for the UK-owned sector.

The major inference from this equation is that the main determinant of sales growth is competitiveness, specifically through unit labour costs and investment. Monopoly power appears to be completely irrelevant in terms of increasing sales, and also research intensity is directly related to growth. Whether this is due to the fact that it is those sectors that are growing that can afford to spend money on Research and development, or whether the results from this expenditure are the so called 'engine for growth' it is not possible to say from this analysis. It is also worth noting that, on average over the period, using the mean value, sales of manufactured goods by UK owned companies increased by only a very small amount in real terms.

Table 6.1e   Dependent Variable SALESi.

Variable	Coefficient	't' value
Constant	−0.22	7.36**
ULCi	−0.22	−6.26**
INV85	0.045	2.07**
RESEARCH	0.015	1.85*
CR5	$-2.1.10^{-5}$	−0.02
METALS[3]	−0.08	−2.29**
VEHICLES	−0.09	−2.00**

Mean of dependent variable 0.188.
$R^2 = 0.59$.   Adjusted $R^2 = 0.51$.

Estimation of the Dynamic Model for the Foreign-Owned Sector

There are two differences in the formulation of the model for the foreign data, in the second equation, it is likely that any change in employment will be related to the conditions faced by the industry as a whole. Therefore, the value of EMPLOYi for the domestic sector is included as an explanatory variable.

Secondly, it also is necessary, in a similar vein to chapter two, to test whether the foreign-owned firms are uniformly distributed across manu-

---

[3] Five industry dummies were used here, metals, chemicals, food and drink, wooden products and vehicles, but only those with significant coefficients are reported.

facturing, with respect to unit labour costs. Thus, the foreign share variable is included in the unit labour costs equation instead of the five firm concentration ratio. One would expect that the foreign-owned firms will be most prevalent where unit labour costs of the foreign sector are lowest, in other words that the relationship between foreign share and unit labour costs is negative.

The results of the estimation of equation 6.3 for the foreign-owned industries:

Table 6.3c   Dependent Variable ULC86.

Variable	Coefficient	't' value
Constant	0.166	4.36**
PROD	$-5.72.10^{-6}$	-4.26**
FORSHARE	-0.13	-1.99**
INV85	-0.008	-1.34
RESEARCH	$0.4.10^{-2}$	0.91
PAY	$1.74.10^{-5}$	3.52**

Mean of the dependent variable = 0.183.
$R^2 = 0.48.$ Adjusted $R^2 = 0.43.$

This equation performs marginally worse than for the UK sample, possibly due to the lack of data on R&D for the foreign-owned sector. Overall however, the results are similar. The most important variables in explaining differences in unit labour costs are again pay and productivity. Given this, it is not surprising that the mean value at the industry level of unit labour costs is lower, albeit not significantly so, than for the UK-owned sample. It should also be noted that there is a negative significant relationship between the foreign share by employment and unit labour

Table 6.3d   Dependent Variable EMPLOYi.

Variable	Coefficient	't' value
Constant	-0.26	-3.95**
SALESi	1.00	14.46**
ULCi	0.27	2.45**
INV86	0.022	0.78
RESEARCH	-0.16	-0.69
EMPLOYi$_d$	-0.41	-2.33**

Mean of the dependent variable = $-0.24.$
$R^2 = 0.78.$ Adjusted $R^2 = 0.76.$

costs in the foreign sector. In other words, foreign firms are not merely concentrated in industries that are most successful, but in those where the foreign sector in particular can keep labour costs down. This would therefore suggest that the relationship between changes in the level of employment in the foreign sector, and changes in unit labour costs will be just as strong as was the case for the domestic sector. This then leads on to the estimation of the employment equation.

Changes in the levels of sales by the foreign-owned sector are clearly the most important determinant of employment in the UK of foreign multinationals, more so than the equivalent variable in the domestic analysis. It is therefore important to focus on the change in the level of sales by foreign firms in the UK over the period. Much of the change in sales by foreign firms may be explained in terms of the global perception taken by some of these firms, so it may be difficult to explain much of the variation across industries in sales by FOEs.

The most startling results here is the extent to which employment in the foreign-owned sector declined over the period. The second point to note is the negative relationship between the change in employment in the foreign owned sector and the industry trend. The model works exceptionally well, with a very high R^2, although much of this is due to changes in the levels of sales. The negative relationship between change in employment by foreign firms, together with the general decline in the foreign sector, would suggest that where UK firms went out of business, the multinationals were able to fill the gap. However, in industries where conditions faced by the foreign firms became too severe, they exercised

Table 6.3e   Dependent Variable SALESi.

Variable	Coefficient	't' value
Constant	0.026	0.15
ULCi	−0.91	−4.45**
INV86	0.015	0.27
RESEARCH	0.55	1.26
CR5	$−1.6.10^{-3}$	−0.48
FORSHARE	0.86	1.31
METALS[4]	−0.34	−1.91*
FOOD	−0.50	−1.98**
VEHICLES	−0.44	−1.91*

Mean of dependent variable −0.0088.
$R^2 = 0.30$.   Adjusted $R^2 = 0.21$.

[4] Again, only the significant dummies are reported.

the option that is only open to firms of a multinational nature, to focus on more profitable markets and to switch production. Unit labour costs again have a positive relationship with employment, suggesting that those firms that have the lowest unit labour costs achieve this through a higher capital/labour ratio and therefore lower employment levels.

This equation does not perform as well for the foreign sector as for the UK one, with the only significant variables here being unit labour costs. It is noticeable also here that the mean fall in sales experienced by the foreign industries is substantially lower than the fall in employment. This may well account for a significant fall in unit labour costs over time. When this is accompanied by an increase in the ratio of sales to employment, one can see that the average number of jobs created by a foreign firm in the UK is likely to be less than for a comparable UK plant. The sales to employment ratio is already greater in the FOEs, so any job creation prospects are diminished even further.

CHANGES IN THE CONFIGURATION OF THE FOREIGN-OWNED SECTOR

Analysis over this time period is complicated by the fact that the nature of the foreign sector was changing, with the increase in the Japanese and European shares, and a decline in US ownership. Thus when looking at wage and productivity issues, in foreign MNEs, it is important to attempt to address this issue, albeit with the restrictions of the limited data available.

Data is available on Japanese employment in manufacturing in the UK (JETRO, 1986).[5] From this it is possible to derive some estimates for the Japanese share of the foreign sector, as well as which industries have experienced an increase in Japanese employment over the period. There were fifteen of the fifty-four industries used here that included Japanese-owned establishments, as at 1986, most notably: industrial electrical equipment, telecommunications and electronic capital goods, consumer electronic goods, and motor cars. Japanese plants when first in operation tend to show low levels of labour productivity due to low levels of value added, resulting from largely the use of the factory to assemble imported components, (Nomura Research Institute 1989). Over time however, as the degree of vertical integration at the plant increases, so does the value added, and hence the estimates of labour productivity.

---

[5] Japanese External Trade Organisation, London.

In order to test therefore, whether the increase in the Japanese presence has an effect at the industry level on wages or productivity, it is necessary to employ a reformulation of equation 6.1. This includes a dummy variable for where the Japanese share of foreign employment has increased, and also a variable for the size of the Japanese share by employment at 1986.

$$PAYi = a_1 + \beta_{111}*PRODLOWi + \beta_{112}*PRODHIGHi + \beta_{12}*UC + \beta_{13}*$$
$$SEASTi + \beta_{14}*FEM + \beta_{15}*FORSHARE + \beta_{18}*FORGROW + \beta_{16}*CR5$$
$$+ \beta_{17}*SIZEi + \beta_{19}*JAPINC + \beta_{119}*JAPSHARE + e_1 \qquad (6.4a)$$

$$PRODi = a_2 + \beta_{21}*PAYi + \beta_{22}*INV85 + \beta_{23}*RESEARCH + \beta_{15}*$$
$$FORSHARE + \beta_{18}*FORGROW + \beta_{16}*CR5 + e_2 \qquad (6.4b)$$

In general, Japanese firms pay lower wages than do other foreign firms, but there is no evidence that this is due to the distribution effect, as none of the industries where Japanese firms operate pay below average wages. It is then possible to determine the extent to which the increased Japanisation of UK manufacturing, together with the retreat of several US manufacturing firms from the UK. The extent to which this has caused the changes over time in the aggregate differential paid by the foreign owned sector, and more importantly, in the foreign effect in these industries, can then be tested. Thus, the estimation of the simultaneous system using equation 6.4a produces the following results (Table 6.4).

These results are very much in line with the previous ones for the foreign sector. However, the most startling one here is that the growth of

Table 6.4a   The Wage Equation.

Variable	Coefficient	't' value
Constant	−0.01	−0.08
PRODHIGHi	0.64	7.35**
PRODLOWi	$-2.0 \cdot 10^{-2}$	−0.09
CR5	0.003	1.97**
SIZE	−0.04	−0.67
FORSHARE	0.03	0.09
FORGROW	0.34	5.54**
UNION	0.61	0.27
JAPSHARE	−1.76	−2.02**
JAPINC	−0.07	−1.53

Mean of dependent variable = 0.24.
(without logit transformation)
$R^2 = 0.84$. Adjusted $R^2 = 0.82$.

Table 6.4b   Productivity Equation.

Variable	Coefficient	't' value
Constant	0.07	0.84
PAY	0.91	5.97**
INV85	0.1	0.53
RESEARCH	0.005	0.27
FORSHARE	0.1	0.4
FORGROW	−0.01	−0.12
JAPINC	0.18	1.74*
JAPSHARE	−0.75	−1.36

Mean of dependent variable = 0.25.
(without logit transformation)
$R^2 = 0.59$. Adjusted $R^2 = 0.53$.

the Japanese sector by industry appears to restrict wage growth, but not productivity growth. There is no evidence to suggest that Japanese firms are anything but more efficient than their domestic counterparts, despite the lower levels of value added initially, and this result is what is being illustrated here, that in time the value added per employee in the Japanese firms rises, while wages do not. Thus, it is likely that as the Japanese-owned sector of industry expands, productivity will rise faster than wages, thus causing an increase in the foreign productivity differential over time, without the corresponding increase in wages. Thus, the wage share in the foreign-owned sector is likely to decline, and the relationship between wages and labour productivity will become weaker.

The future determination of wage rates and wage increases within these plants is then a subject that I do not intend to address any further here. Clearly with better data it would be possible to examine these factors more closely, and obtain a better feel for the different constituent effects involved. Dunning (1986) mentions several of the factors by citing anecdotal evidence, such as the desire of Japanese firms to recruit essentially unskilled workers and train them in the company's methods. This has the effect of generating a high degree of firm specific human capital, which along with the bargaining structures and procedures, will tend to reduce workers' bargaining power. Thus, it would appear that over time the workers advantageous position in terms of bargaining with MNEs, as defined in chapter five, likely is to be eroded. Workers appear less able to gain from such productivity advantages, with the foreign wage differential becoming smaller and the productivity/wage gap increasing.

CONCLUSION TO THE DYNAMIC STUDY

This chapter reiterates the argument that foreign firms do on average have a competitive advantage over domestic producers, not only in terms of a productivity – wage gap, but also in terms of unit labour costs. The distinction here is important, particularly when one uses the concept of value added as a measure of productivity. Japanese plants in the UK for example are characterised by low levels of value added (see the report on the Census of Production, summary volume table 18) particularly when they first commence production. This is not because they are at all inefficient, but because the plants often begin life merely by assembling components imported from the parent company's factories elsewhere. This explains the relatively small increase in labour productivity over the period in the foreign sector.

The model has been estimated over a period when then foreign share of UK manufacturing, measured by employment, fell from 14.5% to 13%. However, the foreign-owned sector accounted for 16.7% of gross value added in 1983, but only 11.6% in 1986. This is a significant result, as it suggests that the sourcing policy of the foreign sector has changed over the period. The composition of the foreign sector changed markedly, even over the short time period. While this is likely to change the distribution of foreign-owned employment away from the regions, it is also likely to change the nature of the jobs, at least in the short term, with more assembly production being carried out.

In the previous chapters, a strong theme has been the 'going rate hypothesis', the constant term in all the wage equations is very strong, suggesting that firm specific factors will merely cause variations around the industry mean, through the factors outlined in the bargaining model. However, this is clearly not the case with the rate of change of wages, as there is never a positive significant constant term. This demonstrates the fact that there is no exogenous force for wages to change, even including inflation, and any wage increase has to be bargained for by the workers. Indeed, the constant term in the wage increase equation for the domestic sector is negative. When this is allied to the result that unionisation appears to have no positive effect on the wage rate in the foreign-owned sector, one can see why the productivity/wage gap for the foreign-owned sector is larger than for the domestic sector.

The results for the foreign-owned sector suggest that those firms with the highest growth in unit labour costs, also have the highest growth of employment, but not sales. One possible explanation for this is that this increase in unit labour costs occurs because it is the firms that carry out the least investment which grow in terms of employment, while investment and research and development induce a reduction in employment. In such cases, this result, demonstrates that it is the most profitable firms that are able to pay for R&D and investment. These firms then generate a capital/labour substitution, while reducing unit labour costs and increasing competitiveness and therefore sales accordingly.

This is very much a product-market lead argument, which links in with the Nash bargaining hypothesis, that wages are positively related to market power in the product market, with unions as well as employers having a strong incentive to maximise the economic rent to the firm. Productivity is then negatively related to unit labour costs, while wages and productivity, (allowing for the plant specific factors) are highly correlated. This ties in with what the conclusions of the previous chapters, that there is most definitely evidence to support the efficiency wage theory, that the most successful firms not only pay the highest wages, but have the highest capital/labour ratios as well.

Clearly, what is presented here is a model where wages are endogenously determined, and given these conditions, the neoclassical model may be true in terms of expansion of the capital stock, but that there is no evidence to suggest that it is true in terms of employment. Given this conclusion, that employment creation is lower in foreign firms than in UK ones, it may be necessary to infer that the employment creation assistance that is made available to prospective investors from abroad, may not be as worthwhile as it at first appears. One of the major factors of course in this would then be from where these firms then obtain their capital goods to generate this expansion. Employment will be created if they are bought from UK firms, but if they are imported, this may only serve to worsen the balance of payments.

It would also appear to be the case that employment in the foreign-owned sector is less stable than in the UK sector, something suggested by Cowling and Sugden (1987) and McAleese and Counahan (1979). This makes intuitive sense, that those firms with the greatest number of options are more likely to exercise them, but without carrying out some more sophisticated analysis on the demand side it is difficult to say more.

REFERENCES

Cowling, K. and Sugden, R. (1987) *Transnational Monopoly Capitalism*. London: Wheatsheaf Books.
Dunning, J.H. (1986) *Japanese Participation in British Industry. London*: Croom-Helm.

Fagerberg, J. (1988) International Competitiveness. *Economic Journal* vol. 98, June, pp. 355–374.

McAleese, D. and Counahan, M. (1979) "Stickers" or "Snatchers"? Employment in multinational corporations during the recession. *Oxford Bulletin of Economics and Statistics*, no. 41 pp. 345–58.

7

Concluding Remarks

GENERAL COMMENTS

The previous six chapters have developed several hypotheses concerning the behaviour of the foreign-owned sector of UK manufacturing industry. This is an area that has been discussed before, although the idea that the foreign sector may be 'different' is generally treated as an afterthought. Once one has established whether foreign firms do pay higher wages, it is necessary to attempt to explain this differential.

The Foreign Wage Differential

There are, as has been demonstrated, many factors that will determine this foreign wage differential, but essentially they can be divided into two. The differential either results from the foreign plants having higher levels of the factors that have a positive effect on wages, or that the majority operate in high-wage industries, or alternatively, that there is something inherently different about the foreign-owned sector. There are many possible firm specific factors that may cause higher wage rates, such as the capital/labour ratio or unionisation. However, one of the most important factors in explaining the foreign mark-up in terms of wages is the extent to which the distribution of the foreign sector of firms is skewed towards the high-wage, high productivity sector. Davies and Lyons (1991), for example state that of the 40% productivity advantage that the foreign sector has, just under half of this is due to the difference in the sectoral distribution of foreign-owned firms compared with domestic ones. This however still means that, when comparing firms in the same industry, labour productivity is over twenty per cent higher in the foreign-owned sector. There are several factors that stand out as being likely causes. The capital/labour ratio for the foreign sector is far greater, and the average plant size for the foreign-owned firms is greater, suggesting gains from economies of scale. Davies and Lyons also cite some possible explanations, such as the *best practice hypothesis*, that those firms that go multinational are those which have some advantage that can be exploited, and this advantage is merely a reflection of it. There are however, several other explanations such as differences in labour skills, in other words the human capital approach, capital inputs, or profitability resulting from market power in the product market. It is therefore impossible in these terms to distinguish between the two broad explanations, human capital theory, and the generic differences possessed by multinationals.

This demonstarates the presence of ownership specific advantages in the foreign sector, and the initial results of chapter two must therefore be seen in this light. While it is possible to show that there is a significant difference between the wages paid by foreign-owned firms and domestic companies at the industry level, it is impossible to determine whether it is an absolute mark-up, or a proportional one. Given this however, there is also the fact that there is a high degree of correlation between foreign and domestic wages across industries. This suggests that one of the most important determinants of wages will be in inter-industry differences.

In order therefore to distinguish between these two possibilities, the index numbers were used to break down the aggregate foreign firm wage differential into the foreign effect and the distribution effect. For the foreign sector as a whole, the aggregate differential is 21% for 1986, using three digit level data, which contrasts markedly with the aggregate productivity differential for the same sample of over 40% (see Davies and Lyons). However, while this result is very much as expected, the more interesting ones are derived when one separates this effect into its component parts. The measure of the foreign effect, given by F_1 and F_2 also provide an insight into the nature of the foreign mark-up in general. F_2 is only negligibly different from one, suggesting that the size of the foreign mark-up is not skewed towards the high productivity (wage) sectors. The hypothesis that the mark-up is an absolute one is more plausible than the hypothesis that β is different from zero in equation 2.1. This is an important result, in that the foreign wage differential is always in terms of a percentage mark-up. It appears here that this is not necessarily the case, that an absolute increment is paid by the foreign firms. Not only is this an important concept in determining why foreign firms should pay above the domestic average, but it also has implications for the rest of this section of the analysis. In such a case, where one assumes that the foreign mark-up is an absolute one, then it could well be argued that F_1 is a more appropriate measure of the mark-up in each industry, suggesting that the average foreign mark-up is nearer to 12%. However, even if one uses this result, using:

Aggregate Effect = Foreign Effect * Distribution Effect (2.3)

Then with F = 1.12, and D = 1.14, we still have the result that over 50% of the aggregate foreign wage differential is due to the fact that foreign firms tend to enter the high-wage sectors. Given that the equivalent figures reported by Lyons and Davies indicated that half of the aggregate productivity differential is due to such a phenomenon, it appears that the difference between the foreign and domestic sectors is as much due to the distribution of firms within the high performance sectors as it is to any inherent advantages held by those firms which become multinationals.

There are many inter – industry factors that cause differences between foreign-owned firms in the UK, as well as nationality differences, as demonstrated in chapters two and three. One of the major themes of this book, with specific reference to the changing nature of the foreign sector, is that it is important not to perceive the multinationals in the UK as a homogeneous block. While the majority of the people employed by foreign multinationals in the UK work for US firms, the nature of the foreign sector has changed markedly over the last twenty years, with the reduction in share of the American plants, and the increase in Japanese and European employment. As can be seen from Table 2.2, the wage differential varies markedly among the firms, depending on country of ownership, and thus with the changing nature of the foreign sector, the influence that the foreign sector will have on UK employment issues will change. For example, in 1986, most of the Japanese-owned production in the UK had relatively low levels of value added and was essentially assembly of imported components. The extent to which this will change over time may well arrest the degree to which agglomeration will occur, both in terms of high and low-level centres, but in several cases, such as the Nissan plant in Washington, studies have shown that value added is significantly greater, and that the levels of technology applied have increased. The extent to whether wages have risen in line with this increase in labour productivity is then a possible point of future research.

A possible conclusion from this is then that the foreign sector, particularly the Japanese-owned plants, may become characterised in a similar way to the older US plants, in terms of wages. However, with patently different working practices and higher levels of labour productivity, such explanations of higher wage rates are most definitely closer to the human capital theories than the bargaining explanations.

As well as nationality differences between firms, Hamill (1982) points out many firm level differences that may exist, as a result of the degree to which the parent company adopts a policy of being closely involved with the day to day activities of its subsidiaries. This is a factor in terms of bargaining structure, that is addressed in chapter five. In more general terms, it is necessary when carrying out a study such as this, that it is important to develop models for the plants within the foreign sector, as well as comparisons between the domestic and multinational firms.

One of the major inter-plant differences is how the plant in question fits into the structure of the parent company. One of the explanations for the existence of large multinational companies is the gains that may be derived from the international division of labour. When new plants are created in a host country, they tend to be used initially as 'screwdrivering' plants, assembling components imported from the source country. This indeed is particularly typical of the new Japanese plants in the UK, particularly with a view to the desire of the Japanese firms to invest in the UK in order to avoid import quotas and tariffs into the EU. It is true to say that many of these plants are then over time upgraded to manufacturing these components as well as assembly. However, the idea of division of labour on an international scale, is still applicable, and must be considered in terms of studying wage rates within foreign-owned plants. While obviously it will be the aim of all firms to keep wages as low as possible, it is easy to demonstrate from this that the extent to which the decision to locate abroad is driven by national wage rates, will be a source of employment instability within the foreign sector, should wage inflation in the UK increase. It is important here however to realise that the key variable from the firm's point of view is labour costs rather than wage rates, which is something that is addressed in chapter six. Again, one of the major tenets in the study of multinational enterprises is that employment levels in host countries are more volatile than in the source country, which is a result of using an international division of labour explanation for the existence of MNEs. There are however, several other explanations for why firms should wish to own manufacturing capacity outside their own country. An evaluation of these derive different implications in terms of predictions for the effects on domestic labour markets. There is for example, evidence that firms in certain circumstances will locate production in areas that already have high levels of industry-related research and development, such as 'Silicon Glen' in

Scotland. The theory is that firms will tend to locate in areas where others have already been successful. While the effects of this type of inward investment on the domestic labour market are clear, overall job creation is limited due to the number of these centres. Despite this, there is a clearly defined relationship between the level of production and the effects on the employees and the prospects for the local labour force. Whether or not the cumulative causation theory is applied, there will be some plants where the technology is more sophisticated, where production is linked to research and new technology, while others will be merely assembling imported components. Linked in with this are the local labour market factors, that is that firms will tend to locate the lowest levels of production in areas where there is a large available labour force, and where wage rates are low, in other words in the regions of high unemployment. This may well then lead to a situation where, with increasing globalisation, some regions will become centres of technological development with high levels of research and development, high levels of new technology being employed, and thus having high wages and productivity.

While it is true that high technology industry does tend to concentrate in specific locations, the gains to the host region in practice of such agglomeration may be less than is imagined. Indeed, if one looks more closely at the Scottish example, it is true that the electronics industry has received a large amount of inward investment, but the outcome in terms of these agglomeration economies is less conclusive. Gross output in electronics in Scotland increased by 400% through the 1980s, essentially as a result of inward investment. Traditionally, these have been US companies coming to Scotland, such as Hoover and Timex, both of who have received a good deal of publicity recently. This trend of inward investment is still continuing, with the Japanese. Mitsubishi Electric for example announced the development of a third plant in Scotland, £12m investment to make air conditioners that will employ 200 people, in addition to the 1500 employed manufacturing televisions and video recorders. This is possibly the best UK example of the agglomeration economies that MNEs hope to derive from locating in such centres, although the issues concerning supplier relations are less clear cut.

Electronics by 1990 accounted for 20% of all Scotland's manufacturing output, and 42% of exports. However, the share of value added in this industry is only 24%, compared with an average for the manufacturing sector of 34%. In addition to this Turok reports that the gap is widening, and that while more electronic goods are being exported from Scotland, the average local content is diminishing. This has two causes, the vertical disintegration of existing firms, which lead to the buying in of more components, and the shift towards final assembly on the part of inward investors.

Local linkages between inward investors and suppliers are more established in Scotland that in any other part of the UK, particularly in the electronics industry. (Hood 1991). Turok (1993) summarises the type of linkages that exist, and outlines the major employment effects that will result. Essentially, these linkages are divided into two: developmental, and dependent.

Developmental linkages involve significant transfer of technology and expertise, and are long term arrangements. This therefore tends to generate high quality secondary employment. Dependent relations are fundamentally sub-contracting agreements, with short term contracts for local firms to produce standard, low tech components. In the second case, the inward investor does not become 'embedded' in the region, and secondary employment is volatile.

This focuses on one of the major themes in the inward investment literature, that where firms are motivated to invest by low labour costs, and capital incentives, the production tends to be low value added, low skill employment, with small indirect effects. This, according to Turok (1993) is definitely the case in Scotland, with overall only about 12% of material inputs being sourced locally, most of which are standard, bulky components, rather than high-tech ones. In addition to this, the inward investors tend to have R&D and marketing functions located elsewhere, and thus technology transfer into Scotland is likely to be severely limited.

Conversely, those areas with high unemployment may experience the reverse, with an ever increasing proportion of employment being in assembly plants with low value added and low wages. This is one of the fears often expressed in relation to the new Japanese plants that are being created in the UK, but this does not appear to be well founded into the longer term. Obviously, the level of production that a plant employs may only be proxied, using variables such as the number of technicians and skilled workers employed, or the capital/labour ratio. This factor has shown up with some success, in that as one would expect, those plants that operate with high levels of technology will have higher wages and productivity, while there is less evidence that this is part of the 'New International Division of Labour', and more dependent on industry specific factors. The 'level' of production, for example, using the human capital explanation is an important part of explaining the differences in prevailing wage rates between plants. The extent then to which, foreign firms exhibit these advantages, through higher skill levels, higher capital/labour ratios, or other factors, will then have a bearing on the extent to which wages are higher through either the higher levels of productivity, or greater bargaining ability that accrues to skilled workers. This therefore contributes at the industry level to addressing the five hypotheses in chapter three, that essentially aggregate foreign differential is a combination of the distribution and ownership explanations, and also that foreign firms do exhibit higher levels of labour productivity on average than do domestic ones. However, what is then necessary is to explain in greater detail why the foreign effect should exist. This is essentially what is set out in chapter three, a model that explains wages and productivity. This is done not only in terms of determining the significance of the foreign effect , but also in terms of determining differences in the two sectors' wage determination processes. While the coefficient on the foreign dummy in equation 3.4 is positive, it is not significant, and thus one can deduce that, while the foreign effect in terms of wages does exist, it is mainly due to factors such as higher rates of productivity. What is more important however is the positive significant coefficient on the foreign dummy variable in the productivity equation 3.4b. The productivity equation for the sample as a whole works extremely well, with an R^2 of 0.76, and yet, even allowing for the greater capital/labour ratios and higher wages found in the foreign sector, the foreign effect is significant. This demonstrates that indeed there is some inherent advantage possessed by multinationals, of the type referred to by Davies and Lyons (1991), derived from such factors as the gains from internalisation or the assimilation of new technology, but that this does not feed through significantly to push up wages.

This study has outlined several of the firm specific factors that are suggested in the theory as being important in the determination of wage rates in the foreign-owned sector.However, one of the major factors that is cited in much of the theoretical work that has never really been tested before, the extent to which firms structure can have an effect at the plant level. Enderwick (1985) for example suggests that the bargaining ability of workers' will be severely impaired by the extent to which a plant forms part of a horizontally integrated structure, given the ability that the firm then has to switch production in order to circumvent any strike threats. With the inverse also being true for vertically integrated firms, one can see the theoretical attractions of this argument, particularly when allied with the hypothesis that foreign firms do have an advantage in bargaining over domestic ones, as any threat simply to relocate is likely to be more credible for a firm that is operating in a host economy merely to minimise the total wage bill. This is something to which has been referred to several times, both in the introduction and in chapter five. This is possibly the main reason for the study of multinational enterprises per se, that they can carry the additional threat in a bargaining situation, to relocate a particular function. Using the formulation of bargaining model one can see that where the threat is perceived as being credible, it does significantly reduce workers' bargaining power. Also, from chapters three and four, it is easy to demonstrate that on average, the wage share is lower in the foreign-owned sector, demonstrating that workers are not able to attain the full benefit of this higher labour productivity.

It would also appear however, that this threat to relocate is no more credible for a foreign firm in the UK than for a domestic one. This intuitively has appeal, due to the fact that foreign plants tend to be larger than the industry average, involving high sunk costs due to the need to acquire information on a foreign market, and high set up costs. As these would be lost should the firm leave the UK, the extent to which an MNE is able to take a global perspective, is at least partly negated by an inability to take full advantage of the information attained.

This argument has been put forward several times, but contrasts with the efficiency wage theory that due to the advantages outlined above, MNEs may pay above the industry average for the host economy. Thus, it is then necessary to distinguish between these two factors, and also to distinguish between those effects that determine wage differentials between the foreign and domestic sectors, and those that explain differences *within* the foreign sector. The result derived here is, that while the degree of vertical integration within the UK has a significant positive effect on wages, there is no such positive relationship between the internalisation variable and the wage rate within the foreign-owned sector. This however is due to the fact that collective bargaining often concerns more than merely wage rates, and thus when this effect is assessed in terms of the bargaining model, a different result is derived.

Not surprisingly, given the estimates of the distribution effect outlined in chapter two, several industry dummies show up as being significant in the determination of plant level wages. This however is more prevalent when assessing the UK-owned sample rather than the foreign sample. There are two industries that have a positive effect on plant level wages within the foreign-owned sector, allowing for differences in the other variables, chemicals and oil. It is interesting that these are significant without effecting the coefficients on the other variables, suggesting that plants within this industry pay higher wages, relative to productivity, than do others. Given the closer the distribution of plants within the foreign sector, across industries, it is perhaps not surprising that the industry effects are less for the foreign sector than as a whole, while there is significant evidence that the prevailing industry wage is one of the most important determinants of the rates offered by foreign plants. This supports the hypothesis that wage determination in the foreign-owned sector, is as dependent on rates of pay being offered by other firms in the industry, as it is by the level of labour productivity within the plant. The extent to which these firms then do pay a foreign mark-up would appear to be dependent on the level of labour productivity, which then links with the human capital explanations, and the level of production and technology employed in the plant, such that the firms are willing to pay above the industry average to attract the best workers, and as part of an industrial relations strategy. The degree to which workers actually bargain up wages, by adopting a confrontational approach when dealing with multinationals appears to be decidedly limited, although there is evidence that workers' bargaining power is influenced by firm structure.

DIFFERENCES AT THE PLANT LEVEL

One of the major differences between the UK and foreign sector plants, is the fact that the average plant size is much greater in the foreign-owned sector. There are essentially two reasons for this, first of all it is likely that the largest, most successful firms are those that become multinational, due to their decision to attempt to service a large market in a foreign location, while many domestic operations aim to service a smaller local market. Secondly, much of the explanation expounded for the reasons why firms invest in manufacturing capacity in a foreign location is based on the desire to gain from economies of scale derived through an international division of labour, for example Casson (1983), Dunning (1985). As with the first explanation, such a rationale is immediately an explanation for why such plants will be greater in size than the industry average. For this reason therefore, a subset of the plant level data base was used, which enabled me to compare forty-two of the foreign plants with a similar set of UK-owned ones. Using this analysis, the foreign effect in terms of wages becomes more pronounced, while it is negligible in terms of productivity, thus suggesting that little of the foreign mark-up in wage rates is due to any increased union militancy due to plant size, while it would appear that the foreign sector is able to derive an advantage over its domestic competitors through scale economies. Thus, again the conclusion is that any foreign mark-up in wages is not due to the workers' ability to increase the wage share, but that the foreign sector tends to use a higher level of technology and thus seeks to recruit employees with higher levels of human capital. This would appear to be born out by the inter-industry comparisons of the foreign/domestic differential, in terms of wages, once size has been corrected for. The constant term in the wage equation for the 'difference' model is positive and significant, again suggesting that there is a foreign effect of approximately thirty pence per hour in terms of wages, correcting for size. At the same time, productivity differences are still important in determining intra-industry as well as inter-industry differences. There is however, no significant difference in productivity levels when correcting for size, the major factor concerning the productivity levels of firms being the capital/labour ratio.

One of the most often studied phenomena concerning the behaviour of the newer foreign firms in the UK is the differences in bargaining structures and working practices that are implemented by these firms. While the Japanese firms have attracted the most attention in recent years, studies of this go back to the work of Gennard (1974). It is well documented that the newer foreign firms tend to favour single-union deals, but the evidence suggests that this is a function of the age of the plant rather than the nationality of ownership, with new UK-owned firms adopting similar procedures. However, with the increasing development of greenfield sites by foreign manufacturing plants in the UK, these issues are going to increase in importance over time, particularly with respect to the growing Japanese sector. The proportion of UK manufacturing that is Japanese-owned is very small, but nevertheless, the differences between the Japanese sector and the older foreign plants is so marked that they are worthy of some discussion. The previous chapter outlined many of these differences, in terms of the relationship between labour productivity and wages. There is a good deal of anecdotal evidence that is cited by Dunning (1986) in his study of some of the Japanese manufacturing plants in the UK, such as their desire to train their own workers, to employ women and to avoid multi-union bargaining. This issue, Dunning reports, stretches further than the issue of unionisation. Japanese firms tend to have 'single status' contracts, such that complete flexibility among the work force is ensured, without any demarcation problems. Together with these 'new' working practices, new bargaining structures are agreed to allow for the voicing of grievances among the work force. Given these changes in the industrial relations structures, it is therefore not surprising that tests for structural change in wage and productivity equations prove significant when looking at the nationality of ownership question in chapter five. Indeed these type of qualitative explanations provide a substantial part of the answer as to why there are structural differences in the equations.

Assessing the behaviour and labour relations practises of foreign-owned firms in general however, causes one to evaluate another strain in the literature, for which support has been found here. This point was first put forward by Cowling and Sugden (1987), and the argument is that, while foreign firms may well pay wages above the industry average, due to changes in working practices increasing work intensity, labour costs do not rise. This is something that is illustrated in chapter five with the bargaining model. While it would appear to be true that the ability of workers to increase wages are greater when dealing with a foreign-owned firm, this is essentially due to the higher levels of profitability that exist in the foreign sector, such that these firms can afford to pay more, without the wage share rising. Indeed, as can be seen from the results concerning unit labour costs in chapter six, ULC is lower in the foreign-owned sector than in the UK one. Not only are unit labour costs lower in the foreign sector, despite the fact that wages tend to be higher, but also that, within the foreign sector, unit labour costs tend to be lowest in those sectors where the foreign presence is greatest. Given the significant nature of the distribution effect in terms of the aggregate wage differential paid by the foreign sector, this clearly demonstrates the greater productivity and efficiency that the foreign firms are able to achieve. Despite the fact that these firms tend to operate in the high-wage sectors, and pay above the industry average, there is still a significant negative relationship between unit labour costs and foreign entry into an industry, despite the obvious positive relationship between wage rates and ULC. One of the major reasons for this is clearly concerned with, again the relationship between wages and productivity, and the level of production employed at the plant level. From the positive significant relationship between unit labour costs and research intensity in the UK sector, one must surmise that these firms that employ a high level of new technology have then to employ a highly skilled work force, which must then be compensated accordingly. It would appear that these higher wages are not matched by the productivity gains in such a situation, where in the foreign sector in general, the productivity differential is greater than the wage differential. From this, it is possible to derive an indication of why the relationship between productivity and wages is segmented in UK manufacturing industry. In general, it would appear that, technological advance is more advantageous in terms of the difference between labour productivity and average wages to the foreign-owned sector. UK plants, it appears, due to the traditional industrial relations procedures, tend to have to increase the number of jobs that are classified as 'skilled' as they improve technologically and thus the wage bill will rise due to skill differentials. Foreign firms in the UK however, suffer from this problem to a lesser degree, particularly in the case of new plants that have the simplified bargaining structures outlined elsewhere, are able to increase levels of labour productivity through the use of new technology, without negating much of this potential improvement in profitability through higher wage claims.

Given the general differences between the typical domestic and foreign-owned plant, one can see that the greater investment intensity in the foreign sector will serve to increase this advantage over time. Again, this fits with the 'appropriability' explanation of Multinationals, that they do posses some inherent advantage that they perceive to be applicable to the foreign market. Given the changing nature of the foreign-owned sector during the time period, the age factor is also likely to derive advantages for the newer plants.

THE BARGAINING ISSUES

Particularly with respect to these newer foreign plants, that tend to be located in the regions, one can explain why the productivity/wage gap is greater using a bargaining model. This also generates the result that the upwards pressure on wages as a result of this increased firm performance is likely to be less than in other areas in the UK.

In addition to this they also suggest that due to the higher levels of productivity and profitability that exist in the foreign-owned sector, higher wages do not necessarily imply greater bargaining power for the workers. This is beacuse a higher proportion of the firms income still accrues to the shareholders. While these results demonstrate that the relationship is not as straightforward as this, one of the strongest results of this work is that the wage differential is not as great as the productivity differential, and that the firms' bargaining power at the plant level where these newer procedures are in place is greater than where they are not.

This approach outlines several marked differences between the foreign and domestic sectors. The way that the model is formulated, it is to be expected that the workers' bargaining power coefficient is likely to be greater in the foreign-owned firms, due to the foreign effect. However, the important results are those concerned with the differences between the estimates of bargaining power for the various sub-samples of the foreign sector. These results are very much as one would expect. The important factors are firm structure, price elasticity of demand in the goods market, and nationality.

The extent to which the plant is part of a vertically integrated firm structure has often been suggested as one of the major factors that will have a positive significant effect on workers bargaining power. The result that has been derived is that, for whatever reason, the share of value added that accrues to workers is greater, where a plant is an important part of an integrated firm structure. This is essentially explained as by the fact that the firm is generally unable to bypass industrial action by switching production between plants, and also the fact that a strike in one location can jeopardise production world wide. The reverse is true for horizontally integrated firms, where worker's bargaining power is reduced due to the negligible effect that a strike can cause in the short term.

There is also evidence that the lack of bargaining power in plants with no union representation is exploited to a greater degree by foreign firms than it is by UK ones, while high degrees of unionisation seem not to have any positive effect on bargaining power. These results would seem to be suggesting that the relative bargaining power between unions and multinationals, would appear to be equal, while the firm is able to gain advantages in the absence of unions.

Finally, in support of the use of the Nash bargaining model, there is evidence that workers' bargaining power is diminished in cases where the price elasticity of demand, as perceived by the firm, is high. Thus, in cases where the firm is not able to pass on its costs to the consumer, it is more likely to resist wage demands, while unions understand this resistance. The other major difference using the formulation of the bargaining model expressed in equation 5.25, in terms of the important determinants of bargaining power, are the results that national level bargaining agreements tend to favour foreign firms in the UK, but act in the interest of unions when dealing with UK-owned plants. The essential reason for this, is that where a foreign firm owns several manufacturing plants in the UK, then the industrial relations structures are essentially formulated by the firm, for example the 'Blue Book' agreement that Ford UK has with the unions. These are formulated in the interest of the firm, to allow for a high degree of co-ordination of the firms industrial relations policies, particularly if they are being closely monitored by the parent company. Hamill (1982) for example claims that the extent to which parental control is exerted will limit union power, as local management have scope to claim that they are unable to agree to certain demands.

Also, the existence of national level bargaining, is likely to provide an advantage to the firm, as the capacity for the firm to co-ordinate its activities is likely to be greater than that of disparate unions. In the case of a uni-national domestic firm however, it is more likely that the unions will be able to assimilate a higher percentage of firm level information, and co-ordinate their activities. This will enable the union to gain advantages not open to workers bargaining with a MNE, who, in the final analysis, have the additional threat simply to relocate away from the UK. Such a scenario may be particularly likely if the firm perceives the profitability of their whole UK operation to be threatened by wage demands.

While the bargaining analysis that is used here has produced many interesting results, and affirmed many hypotheses that thus far do not appear to have thoroughly tested, there is the alternative approach that is based upon human capital or productivity. Foreign firms have certain advantages over the domestic sector, which then accounts, through higher levels of productivity, for the higher wages paid. The central conclusion in this work is that neither explanation on its own is sufficient, in that explaining inter-plant wage differentials within the foreign sector, bargaining power is important, while in general structural differences account for the foreign effect. In terms of a comparison of these two theories, it has become apparent that the human capital/productivity explanation can be used to account for the inter-plant differences between the foreign and domestic sectors. The results derived in chapters three and four suggest that the foreign sector has on average, greater investment intensity and larger plant size, as well as the individual plants being more integrated into the global structure of the firm. It is therefore these, and similar factors that generate the greater levels of labour productivity that pervade in the foreign-owned sector, with above average wages being a result.

However, when assessing inter-plant differences within the foreign sector, the results suggest that the relative bargaining abilities of the workers and management are important. While the 'going rate hypothesis' can be used to explain some of the intra-industry divergence between wages and productivity, the results from chapter five indicate that there are several phenomena, such as unionisation, firm structure, location, and the nature of the product market, that are extremely important in determining wages through the bargaining framework. Given the heterogeneity of the foreign-owned sector, and the fact that to a large extent the foreign firms take account of industry average wages, this then derives an explanation for why the relationship between labour productivity and wages is so weak for foreign MNEs in the UK.

This heterogeneity in the foreign-owned sector has increased over time, particularly as the proportion of Japanese and European-owned firms has increased. While the Japanese-owned sector is extremely small in terms of the total UK employment, it is important from an analytical respect for two reasons.

1. The major differences in terms of the nature of employment, working practices and technology in these plants.
2. The large importance that these plants have attached to them with respect to their host local economies, such as the North East of England and South Wales.

This then outlines the major differences between the Japanese plants and the older US-owned ones, not only in terms of working practices, but also in terms of the relationship between wages and productivity. While value added/employment is low during the first years of the plants' life, the wage share is low due to the fact that wages are low. Chapter four proposes several reasons for why wages in these plants tend to be low, such as the high rates of local unemployment, institutionally low levels of union bargaining power, and low levels of skilled workers, with firms looking to generate high levels of specific human capital through their own training programmes.

What has been demonstrated in chapter six is that in virtually every case, wages do not rise as fast as productivity, and thus given the large labour productivity increases in these plants, the wage share diminishes over time. Also, with Japanese plants basing wages on the going rate of the local economy, the relationship between wages and productivity is likely to diminish over time.

SUMMARY OF RESULTS

One of the central treatises in the study of MNEs is that put forward by Hymer (1972), concerning the extent to which these firms contribute to the accumulation of capital in certain locations, with other regions being consigned to merely assembly operations. While there is clearly evidence that certain locations are characterised by high levels of technological activity linked to production, such as 'Silicon Glen' in Scotland, there is little evidence that this is part of a global strategy by firms to locate in these areas to the detriment of the others. While there is evidence that the cumulative causation theory has a good degree of credence, with some locations having a high degree of technological activity linked to manufacturing, there are so few of these centres that while the reasons for firms to locate in these centres, it is impossible with the bounds of this study, to examine, the effects on the peripheral regions. Such phenomena are also linked to the hierarchic ideas of Enderwick (1985), that a firm employing the division of labour will tend to locate high-level production in certain areas, with the 'screwdrivering' plants elsewhere.

In addition to this, in the past few years there has emerged evidence that new foreign-owned plants are tending to follow one another to particular locations, such as South Wales. The issue here however is which factors determine the decisions for firms, particularly foreign ones, to set up plants in a particular location, with respect to the different incentives on offer. This, however, is not an issue that cannot be addressed with the data available, within the confines of this study.

A subject that has attracted a good deal of attention in the industrial relations literature, with respect to the behaviour of the new foreign plants in the UK, is the difference between the new Japanese plants and the older UK and indeed US-owned plants. The percentage of UK employment that is accounted for by Japanese plants is exceptionally small, and the WIRS database does not provide sufficient data on the Japanese plants. There is a good deal of work being carried out on this question, and it is clear that, through the age effect and the differences in the productivity and wage rates, there are differences between the Japanese owned and other foreign sectors. However determination of the causes of these differences, is not the aim of this book.

Similarly, much of the work is presented here in terms of the differences between multinational and uni-national firms. It would have been desirable therefore to be able to divide the sample into three sections, UK MNEs, foreign MNEs and UK domestic firms. Unfortunately, this requires some firm level information concerning the ownership of manufacturing capacity overseas, on the part of the UK firms. This idea however is most certainly a possible avenue of future research, determining the extent to which MNEs behave differently in their source country, than do uni-national firms. The purpose of studying MNEs per se, is the fact that their options vis a vis the location of manufacturing capacity are greater. While it is postulated that UK MNEs operating in Britain are in some way tied to the UK, and thus behave within the UK as any other British firm, there are many examples where this has turned out not to be the case, with possibly the best example of a UK MNE closing home-based capacity rather than overseas operations is that of Tate and Lyle.

The incentives given to foreign firms are greater than to domestic firms, but if it is the case that these UK firms also take a global perspective, the UK is in competition for this investment, in the same way as it is for, say, a Japanese car plant.

Secondly, once established, these plants have characteristics common to the foreign-owned sector rather than the domestic one, with correspondingly high levels of labour productivity and a low wage share.

Data that enables the sample to be divided into three in this way would be a useful addition to a study of this type. MNEs tend to carry out a high percentage of research and development in their source country, and thus one could test whether this R&D being closely linked to production has a positive effect on productivity and wages. However, in order to carry out any in depth study on this 'third group', one would need to know whether these plants were created to take advantage of the international division of labour, and the extent of horizontal integration within the firm. It is only when one is able to distinguish between these separate the factors that that an explanation of plant level differences in wage rates can be attained.

Given all that has been said concerning technological agglomeration and the relationship between labour market factors and the links between R&D and production, it is unfortunate that there is no data available concerning R&D expenditure in the foreign-owned sector at the industry level, or in the WIRS study. In the UK sector, clearly there is a relationship between labour productivity growth and R&D, and therefore it would be desirable to determine the extent to which R&D expenditure in the foreign sector has on the various labour market issues. One would imagine that the more R&D is linked to production in the foreign-owned sector, the more labour productivity will increase, with wages only rising by a proportion of this productivity gain, and the wage share being reduced. With the wage share diminishing over time, and the likely capital/labour substitution that follows successful R&D, then the question for policy makers changes. The potential benefit to the UK economy from this investment would have to be assessed in terms of the extent to which technological advance is diffused in to the UK sector, rather than in terms of direct employment effects. Given the lack of a relationship between the foreign share and labour productivity in the UK-owned plants, this diffusion appears to be negligible. Thus, the benefits from this high level production would extend no further than the jobs created, which then begs the question of whether these firms in the long term do generate employment in the UK, or cause an employment substitution away from the UK sector.

Evidence is emerging that inward investment in the UK tends to lead to employment substitution, away from established firms and towards the new investors. Fords[1] have complained that due to the advantages that the Japanese have of operating a new greenfield site, established firms are having to shed labour in order to compete. This, they claim, has serious implications for future R&D in the motor industry, as not only were 1180 manufacturing jobs to be shed in 1993, but also 262 staff jobs.

One of the continuing themes through this study is that of the 'going rate hypothesis', and so, it would be interesting to test whether this phenomenon is present in other host countries.

Final Summary and Concluding Remarks

The main issues here revolve around the relationship between wages and productivity, particularly for the foreign-owned firms. In most previous studies where productivity is used to explain variations in wages, in a neoclassical framework, it is assumed that workers are paid according to the marginal product of labour, with efficiency then determining firm or plant size. What is demonstrated is that neither a confrontational bargaining approach, or a simple productivity based approach are sufficient for explaining inter plant differences in wage rates. While this is especially true for the foreign sector, it can also be demonstrated for the UK-owned sector. In every formulation of the wage equation in chapters three, four and six, the constant term is significant. This illustrates that there is some inherent median value of wages per hour, around which actual plant level rates will vary according to the bargaining, productivity and other factors outlined.

This factor is even more important in terms of explaining plant level variations in the foreign sector, where the relationship between wages and labour productivity is even more complex. The major determinant of inter-plant differences in wage rates in the foreign-owned sector, appears to be the industry average, with the foreign mark-up then being determined by the various other factors, such as productivity and unionisation. Thus, two foreign plants in the same industry, with great differences in labour productivity, are likely, ceteris paribus to have much smaller differences in wage rates. This is something that is supported by the results from the equation with a slope dummy included for high produc-

---

[1] House of Commons Select Committee on Employment, 10th March 1993.

tivity. This is an important explanation of why wages do not follow productivity, but it also demonstrates, that wages in the foreign-owned sector are centred around some mean. However, when allowing for this the relationship between wages and labour productivity is significant. This is similar to the result that is outlined in chapter six, concerning the relationship between wage and productivity growth.

In terms of wage growth, the results from chapters four and six demonstrate briefly the effect that a high foreign presence can have on the domestic sector. Chapter two decomposes the aggregate foreign wage differential into it's component parts. Even allowing for the distribution effect, one can demonstrate that increased foreign ownership in an industry, which tends to pay higher wages, tends to cause bidding up of wages in the domestic sector. This clearly has severe implications for the wage share, and therefore the profitability of the domestic sector.

As is said above, very little has been written on the determinants of the wage share in manufacturing. The wage share is often seen as merely a combination of the factors that determine wages and productivity. However, the concept of the wage share is important, given the significant evidence that it is the wage share, or the wage bill that is at issue in the bargaining situation. Also, the use of a wage share equation in this study, allows one to test several hypotheses concerning the effects of foreign-owned firms. Clearly, the wage share is bid up by the presence of foreign firms, and this causes the wage share to increase. Also, it is possible to demonstrate that, while the age effect is not significant in terms of wages or productivity separately, when assessed in terms of the wage share, it demonstrates the advantage that appears to accrue to newer plants. Given that on average the foreign sector is not as old as the domestic sector, this further underlines the advantage that the foreign sector has. Finally, the heterogeneity of the foreign-owned sector of the UK manufacturing sector is stressed, when looking at issues concerning the effects on the labour market conditions, it is important to take this into account. It is hard to envisage for example, Japanese plants, that tend to pay below-average wages, causing a bidding up of rates of pay in the UK sector. However, the Japanese inward investors that have received most attention in the UK are located in low wage areas, such as South Wales and the North East of England, so a similar effect may still present itself on a local scale.

The major policy issue to which this study is of relevance is that of the investment incentives that are offered in order to attract foreign firms into the UK. Such incentives usually take the form of tax 'holidays', direct grants, or exemptions from business rates.

There are essentially two reasons given by bodies such as the Welsh Development Agency and local development corporations, as to why such payments are available. Firstly, that such investment creates employment, and secondly that it encourages the introduction of new technology into the UK.

While clearly, the building of a new plant is always going to generate employment, this study has shown that such investment tends to be more capital intensive than the indigenous sector, and thus less employment is generated than may be imagined. Also, while there is evidence that these foreign firms do have higher levels of new technology than older plants, there is little evidence that this is diffused through the industry. Certainly, there is no evidence that a significant presence of foreign-owned capacity in a particular industry has any positive effect on the levels of labour productivity in the rest of the industry.

This would suggest therefore that a large proportion of these incentives is being given to firms who already posses an ownership advantage of some type, and serve therefore merely to increase advantages over domestic competitors.

While clearly public agencies in other countries are willing to pay similar incentives, then they need to be available in order to attract new investment into the UK. However, given the results concerning the employment policies of foreign as opposed to UK-owned firms, one has to question the degree to which of these incentives should be available only to foreign investors.

REFERENCES

Casson, M.C. (1983) *The Growth of International Business*. London: Allen and Unwin.

Cowling, K. and Sugden, R. (1987) *Transnational Monopoly Capitalism*. London: Wheatsheaf Books.

Davies, S.W. and Lyons, B.R. (1988) 'Theories of Horizontal Multinational Enterprise'. University of East Anglia mimeo.

—— (1991) Characterising relative performance: The productivity advantage of foreign-owned firms in the UK. University of East Anglia Economics Research Centre discussion paper no. 9106.

Dunning, J.H. – (1985) (1985) *Multinational Enterprises, Economic Structure and International Competitiveness*. Wiley/IRM. Geneva.

—— (1986) *Japanese Participation in British Industry. London*: Croom-Helm.

Enderwick, P. (1985) *Multinational Business and Labour*. London Croom-Helm.

Gennard, J. (1974) 'The impact of foreign-owned subsidiaries on host country labour relations: The case of the UK'. In *Bargaining Without Boundaries*. (ed. Flanagan, R.J. and Weber, A.R.) The University of Chicago Press.

Hamill, J. (1982) 'Labour Relations in Foreign-Owned Firms in the UK.' PhD thesis submitted to Paisley College.

Hood, N, (1991) Inward investment and the Scottish economy: Quo Vadis? *Royal Bank of Scotland Review*, no. 169 pp. 17–32.

Hymer, S.H. (1972) 'The multinational corporation and the law of uneven development.' *In Economics and World Order*. (ed Bhagwati, J.N.).

Turok, I. (1993) Inward investment and local linkages: How deeply embedded in 'Silicon Glen' ? *Regional Studies* vol. 27.5 pp. 401–17.

APPENDIX 1
The Data for The Plant Level Study

The plant level data is collected from the Workplace Industrial Relations Survey for 1984, as I have said elsewhere. From this I extracted 427 manufacturing plants, 72 of which are foreign-owned, mostly USA, still by far the most represented of foreign investors in the UK.[1]

Estimate of Labour Productivity

Unfortunately, the data set does not have good labour productivity data, and so it is proxied by the following:

PROD = SALES *(VA/S)/EMPLOYMENT

VA/S is the (4 digit) industry level measurement of value added/sales, for either the foreign or domestic sector, as is relevant.

The MANPAY variable is the mean wage paid to manual workers at the plant.

PROD is labour productivity, as defined above. As I have already said, there is a positive correlation between wages and productivity, and so one would expect a positive significant coefficient here, although more so for the domestic sector.

UNION is the percentage of workers covered by a trade union. This is possibly the best proxy for union power, and therefore one would expect a positive relationship between this and wage rates.

---

[1] see chapter 2.

147

FEMALE is the percentage of full time manual workers that are women. Historically, women workers have been paid less than their male counterparts, and therefore one would expect the coefficient to be negative. There is however, the possibility that this is offset by the industry dummies, there are specific industries that employ a high percentage of women, such as clothing and textiles, and so therefore the industry effect may be stronger here than any inter plant differences across industries.

INTERN is a dummy variable for whether the majority of output is sold to other subsidiaries of the parent company. The expected coefficient here is positive, although as I shall show later, the degree of vertical integration may be more important in terms of union bargaining power that prevailing wage rates.

SKILL is the percentage of manual workers that are classed as skilled. The expected sign here is positive, for two reasons. Firstly, a human capital explanation would be sufficient to explain the higher wages paid to skilled workers over unskilled, and secondly there are often agreements between unions and firms concerning differentials paid to skilled workers.

SEAST is a dummy variable for whether the plant is located in the South East of England. Again the expected sign is positive, to allow for the higher cost of living in the south east, it is reasonable to expect that firms pay more merely to keep their staff.

In addition to these, I also included several dummy variables, as, particularly in the case of new foreign-owned firms, it is believed that the prevailing industry rates of pay will have a bearing on the settlements reached.

OIL refers to the oil industry,
CHEM to the chemicals industry,
CLOTH to the footwear and clothing sectors,
PRINT to the printing and publishing sector.

Estimation of Capital Stock

The CAPITAL variable here is an estimation of the capital/labour ratio, using the following to calculate estimates of the capital stock.
Using industry-level data:

$Q_i = w_i . L_i + r_1 K_1,$

where

Q_i = Value added in industry i.
w_i = wage rate, in industry i.
L_i = employment in industry i.
K_1 = capital stock.
r_1, the rate of return for each industry can then be calculated from:
$r_1 = (Q_i - w_1 . L_i)/K_i$

and then using the firm-level data, for each firm j, it follows that:

$K_j = (Q_j - w_j . L_j)/r_1$ [2]

The STEC variable is the proportion of senior technicians to manual workers. This again may be seen as an indication of the level of technology employed by the firm, as plants that have a high degree of mechanisation will also have more technicians employed.

---

[2] While I accept that this method of estimating capital stock values can be open to criticism, it does derive some values similar to published capital stock data for similar size companies, and as can be seen from the results, works well when applied. There is then a possibility of a spurious correlation between PROD and CAPITAL, but this however is not as serious as may be imagined:
I have defined PRODj, firm level productivity as

PRODj = (Rj – Qi/Ri)/Lj where R refers to revenue

and

Kj . (Qj – wjLj)/ri

and therefore PRODj is being explained by

Ki . (Qj – wj.Lj)/(Qi – wiLi)

it is therefore possible that in cases where the firm is representative of the industry, and

Qj – wjLj

is of similar magnitude to

Qi – wiLi.

Then the firm level labour productivity is being explained by Ki, the industry level value for the capital stock. This is not a particularly large problem however, as we are referring to a typical firm, and so this typical firm is being represented by the typical value of the capital stock. I accept that this is less desirable than using all plant level data, but as this does not exist, I feel that the methodology I have employed is an acceptable alternative.

APPENDIX 2
The Data for The Bargaining Model

The definition of profits used in the expressions above is: REVENUE – WAGE COSTS – OVERHEADS. Unfortunately, WIRS does not have explicit data for overheads, so what is used as a proxy here is non-wage employments costs, essentially salaries of the managerial and clerical workers.

Formation of the Equation

Thus the solution can be generated by maximising the following:

$$U = (WE - W_mE_j)^\gamma (R - WE - H)^{1-\gamma} \qquad (5)$$

with respect to wage rates.

$$dU/dW = E.\gamma (WE - W_mE_j)^{\gamma-1} (R - WE - H)^{1-\gamma} +$$
$$(1-\gamma)(-E)(WE - W_mE_j)^\gamma (R - WE - H)^{-\gamma} = 0 \qquad (6)$$

dividing through by $(WE - W_mE_j)^{\gamma-1}.E.(R - WE - H)^{-\gamma}$
generates:

$$WE = W_mE_j + \Pi^*. \gamma \qquad (7)^1$$

Where $\Pi^* = \Pi/(1 - \gamma)$.

---

[1] An indentical result can be obtained by maximising joint utility with respect to the wage bill.

It is equation 7 that gives the wage bill, weighted by employment, as a function of the industry average and the profits of the firm. In other words the extent to which workers are successful in gaining a mark up on wages over the average, as a function of the profits of the firm.

This can then be estimated directly or it is then also possible to replace γ with $\gamma(Z)$ where Z is the set of variables believed to influence bargaining power: The derivation of these variables is discussed below.

This method of using prevailing wage rates to calculate estimates of γ generates a specific type of measure of bargaining power. The relationship between productivity and wages is already well documented, and so it is important to realise that one sides willingness to concede (i.e. more successful firms paying more or employees in firms that are doing badly being willing to forgo a pay increase to protect their jobs) may well be as important a factor in determining γ, as any strategic moves that either side can make. It is also possible that for firms that pay below average wages, the measure of γ is less than zero.

The point of interest here is the differences in bargaining power, when comparing UK and foreign-owned companies. The formulation of this model also has another distinct advantage, in that it is possible to explain almost all the differences in bargaining power in terms of firm-specific variables, as much of the inter-industry differences will be accounted for by the $W_m E_j$ term.

Variables for the Bargaining Model

The following variables are therefore included.

MANTOT – plant size, measured by the number of manual workers.

STRIKE – a dummy variable for whether the latest wage bargain was settled only after a strike.

REGUP – the unemployment rate in the region local to the plant.

PLANTNEG – a dummy variable for whether there is plant-level bargaining.

NATNEG – a dummy variable for whether there is national bargaining.

INTERN – a dummy variable for whether the plant is part of a vertically integrated firm structure.

HORIZ – a dummy variable for whether the plant is part of a horizontally integrated firm structure. This is proxied by all those plants that are part of a firm structure, but not vertically integrated firms, so may include some 'conglomerate' firms.

FEMALE – the proportion of manual workers that are women.

UNION – union coverage, the proportion of workers covered by a collective bargaining agreement.

MARKET – this is a variable which measures the firms perception of it's market power. It is the degree, in percentage terms that it believes sales would fall following a 5% increase in price.

APPENDIX 3
The Data for The Dynamic Study

The only data that I use here is taken from the Census of Production for 1983 and 1986, and from the CENTRAL STATISTICS OFFICE data sheets that provide similar 3 digit industry level data for the foreign-owned sector only. In addition, union coverage data at the industry level and the percentage of operatives that are women is reported in the New Earnings Survey. In addition, research and development expenditure at the industry level for UK manufacturing for 1985 is reported in a Business Monitors paper.

The two variables that are likely to change merely through inflation are rates of pay and productivity. However, as the analysis concerns the differences in changes across industries, it is not necessary to correct for inflation. Also, it concerns wage increases that are paid, and clearly these are agreed as nominal figures rather than real ones. Several variables are included as levels rather than changes, as in the previous equation. The levels of union coverage, and percentage of women employed are bargaining type variables in themselves, and so have more value if included in this way. Inflation over the period averaged 4.6%, so one wages would be expected to increase by around 15% over the period. It is also however worth noting that any wage increases over the period will have been agreed against the background of large scale contractions in the manufacturing sector over the period, and so one could well infer that wage increases at this time are unlikely to be significantly greater than inflation, and indeed may be lower.

The Rate of Change Variables

The variables used are then calculated to be industry average change between 1983 and 1986 as follows:

$$\text{rate of change for industry i} = \frac{1986_i \text{ value} - 1983_i \text{ value}}{1986_i \text{ value}}$$

The use of the 1986 value as the deflator may not appear logical at first sight, but the reason is that one of the explanatory variables used is the rate of change in the foreign share over the period. Thus, any industries that had a very low foreign share by employment in 1983, could well show a vast increase in the growth of the foreign sector for only a small increase in employment over the three years.

Index

157

For Product Safety Concerns and Information please contact our EU representative GPSR@taylorandfrancis.com Taylor & Francis Verlag GmbH, Kaufingerstraße 24, 80331 München, Germany

Batch number: 08153776

Printed by Printforce, the Netherlands